Picture Framing & Wall Display

By the Editors of Sunset Books and Sunset Magazine

Lane Publishing Co., Menlo Park, California

Closely clustered, generous-scale oil paintings form a pleasing configuration.

This book opens with color photographs chosen to inspire you with framing and display ideas that range from traditional to surprising. All manner of subjects are shown, from folk art to photographs, children's art to prized collections. Included are simple cross-section sketches showing the components used in many of the frames. Because the techniques for making frames and mounting art are similar in many instances, we have avoided repetition by covering general information and techniques in the back of the book in a section entitled "Framing Your Picture."

In preparing this book, we have received the help and cooperation of many home owners, galleries, and frame shops. We are grateful to all of them. In particular, we thank Greg and Nanci Fremstad, Frame Art Workshop; Bernard Hern, Hern Gallery & Frame Shop; Ells and Mimi Marugg; and Paula Kirkeby, Smith-Anderson Gallery. Also, for his editorial help on several sections of this book, our thanks to Sherman Grant.

We also wish to thank Eastman Kodak Company for the photographs credited to individual photographers on pages 7, 8, 9, 23, 24, 25, and 27.

Supervising Editor: Dorothy Krell

Staff Editors: Don Rutherford
Kathryn L. Arthurs
Susan Warton

Design: Tim Bachman

Photography: Darrow Watt
(unless otherwise noted)

Illustrations: Rik Olson

Cover: Array of pictures includes, clockwise from top, Japanese woodcut with linen mat; Peruvian embroidery in flat, gold-leafed frame; photographic print in floater; and two miniature oil canvases in wood frames with liners.

Editor, Sunset Books: David E. Clark

Second Printing June 1980

Simple frames and compatible colors knit this group together—each picture enhancing the others.

Clear primary colors of this painting by Sam Francis glow through the transparent acrylic.

CONTENTS

A GALLERY OF FRAMING & DISPLAY IDEAS

Welcome to our picture gallery. Here and on the upcoming pages, we've collected nearly 100 color photographs for your idea-gathering pleasure. These show examples of what other people have put on the wall, the mats and frames that enhance their choices, and the ways they have displayed the final results to best advantage.

We open the door with a series of wall arrangements—including informal clusters of pictures, symmetrical groupings, and single works judiciously placed to attract the eye.

Further along, you'll see examples from the multitude of frame styles and mat materials available today. Notice the way tones, sizes, shapes, and textures interweave visually to bring subjects to life.

If you are looking for novel notions of what to frame, you're almost certain to find some that you hadn't considered: poster-scale enlargements of dramatic photographs, colorful masks or hand-woven garments discovered abroad, even a splashy masterpiece that comes home from kindergarten.

Also included are special frames to craft yourself for a distinctive look—frames painted, beribboned, studded with mosaic, plushed with fabric.

Let these pages help as you juggle the subjective intangibles that go into framing—which molding to choose, how the tone of a mat will affect the mood of a watercolor, whether your wall wants a brilliant square of fabric or a black and white print. While you may not find here an exact reflection of your taste and needs, you'll find plenty to inspire you.

Harmony from botany ▶
Glints of orange and gold in these botanical prints mirror the warm color of the wall. Their perfect symmetry harmonizes with the rather formal feeling of the room they decorate.

◀ Elegant wraparound for a stairwell
Evoking thoughts of an Oriental screen, Galen Garwood's paper collage envelops you as you reach the second floor landing. Overhead track lights flood the mural-like abstract, which was specially commissioned and custom framed to fit this wall.

...display

The impact of inches
A gentle dose of asymmetry in its placement over the mantel heightens the impact of this portrait of Korea's first monarch. By drawing our eyes slightly to the left, the painting holds its own amid strong architectural features that might otherwise compete too severely. At the same time, the off-center position leaves a narrow shaft of wall for the candelabra.

▼

Dramatic display for icons ▶

Vertical clustering gives this group of Greek and Russian icons the drama of a single, grand-scale work. The effect required careful planning. Mountings and frames are covered in silk of warm-to-cool colors, chosen to enhance both individual icons and the group as a whole. The interlocking arrangement was worked out with paper patterns, then transferred to plywood, which was precisely cut around the arrangement's irregular shape to make a backing for the entire group. Edges of backing were covered with light brown silk. With icons bolted in position, the backing now hangs on heavy wire from the ceiling. Design: Alexander Girard.

A face you won't forget

Centered low in a brightly lighted alcove, this haunting portrait rivets our attention. A provocative focal point, the photograph nevertheless blends harmoniously with its quiet, Mexico-inspired surroundings.
▼

CARL MASER

7

...display

High-level highlight ▶

Sometimes proportions as much as design destine a picture for a particular place. Here a framed and silk-matted Japanese kimono stencil exactly fits width of a doorway and calls attention to the alcove.

LEE ALLYN PARK

Balanced composition ▶

Five pictures of different sizes work together here to compose one pleasing configuration. Good balance, with the largest picture at the hub, seems to stabilize the arrangement. Hung low on the wall, the pictures merge visually with the love seat below.

◄ Symbiosis in silver
Suspended by invisible but herculean fishing line, Mary Tift's silkscreen is set off by the silvery sheen of the mirrored wall behind it, while giving the eye a pleasing pause in the shiny expanse.

LEE ALLYN PARK

◄ A family gathering
Oval shapes mingling with angular, a galaxy of ornate frames adds to the sentimental charm of very-old-to-recent family photographs.

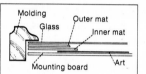

Molding
Glass
Outer mat
Inner mat
Mounting board
Art

▲
Four distinct moods for Dürer's "Young Field Hare"
Across these two pages, Albrecht Dürer's popular watercolor appears in four different guises.

Above, the hare crouches in the darkest field—a wide mat that crops the print closely, paired with a strong inner mat.

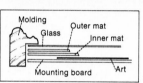

Molding
Glass
Outer mat
Inner mat
Mounting board
Art

▲
Hare seems poised for flight
Balancing a heavier, more ornate frame than the first, the pale mat shown here gives Dürer's water color a completely different feeling. The hare looks freer, ready to bound away. Even so, the dark inner mat restrains it just enough, and accents the warm brown tones.

Frame styles... many ways to go

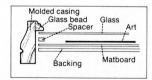

Molded casing
Glass bead
Spacer
Glass
Art
Backing
Matboard

Simple celebration of Mexican folk art ▶
Looking festive against the color of a warm summer sky, this Mexican bark painting gains further glory from the rich antique finish of its simple frame. To make this type of builder's molding frame, consult page 94.

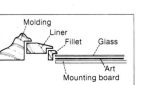

▲ Color and texture "domesticate" the creature

Housed here inside a liner covered with warm brown suede, and doubly fenced by frame and fillet, this hare appears less wild than the creature shown in the other three treatments.

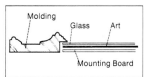

▲ Hare surrounded by deep, dark wood

Heavy, glossy, very dark, and perfectly simple, this frame has no mat, liner, or fillet. The weighty frame might overpower the delicate watercolor if it weren't for the crisp gold of its beveled inner edge, which helps to ease the constraint.

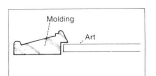

◄ Inverted frame brings art closer to view

This wide frame slopes out from the wall, projecting its subject into the room. The frame's warm finish works with a narrow white mat to highlight the soft tones of the oil still life.

...frames

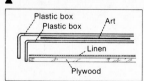

Handled with care

Apparently suspended in thin air, this delicate Harold Paris collage casts a beautiful ragged shadow from its deckle edge. A double plastic box holds the art forward from the linen backdrop. Chemically inert, the plastic will not damage the handmade paper. Design: Plasteel Frames.

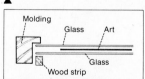

Inside the frame, the wall is the mat

While a heavier treatment might have subdued the spirit of this drawing, a floating frame gives it the breathing space it needs. The art is pressed between two sheets of glass large enough to create a transparent boundary. The wall surface shows through this space.

Military review in red and blue

Brisk and tartan-bright as soldiers themselves, a quartet of passe partout frames spruces up the wall. Narrow inner mats and taped rims create double red stripes around each blue mat. This simple, low-cost, but very effective method of framing is explained on page 100.

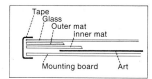

Breaking up angles

Arches, ovals, and other curved shapes require special equipment to achieve—and must be specially ordered. Even so, a break in the angularity rule refreshes the eye and can add romance to a soft and fluid painting like this oil on canvas board.

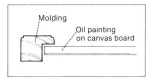

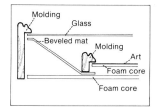

Frame within a frame ▶

A pair of frames (each made of cap-on-stem walnut molding with gold fillet) combined with a deep, beveled mat of suede draws the eye to the sharp perspective in this painting. Both style and finish harmonize with the subject's shadowy-to-bright gradation of values.

Mats matter... make the most of them

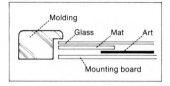

Circles make a happy ▶ change of pace

The plump pumpkins in Toni Carner's harvest scene look ready to roll right into the room through their circular window. The design of this print made a curved mat opening mandatory—but for a refreshing change of pace, consider the circle whenever shapes in a picture comply.

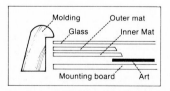

Linen . . . for a hint of texture ▶
A fibrous, oatmeal-color linen mat repeats the grainy texture and underscores the autumnal feeling of this woodcut by Japanese artist K. Saito. An inner mat painted orange, draws attention to the vibrant but minute persimmons scattered at the top of the print.

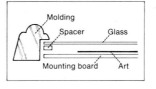

◄ Just enough mat to peek through a deckle edge

Wide, pristine-white, and signed by the artist, Theodora Varney Jones's handmade paper deserves as much notice as her etching at its center. For this reason, the entire sheet floats on the surface of the mat, which sets off the delicate deckle edge with a narrow rim of complementary blue gray.

Color cooperation using double mats

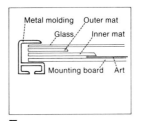

Gentle gradations of color intensity characterize both of these Elton Bennett serigraph prints. Within the metal frame of each, a wide mat echoes the dominant hue, amplifying its value, while a narrow inner mat strengthens the secondary color.

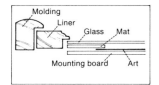

Paired by one mat

Prancing together with twice the spirit that individual frames would allow, wild ponies by Navajo artist Kai-Sa are paired by one buff-color mat.

...mats

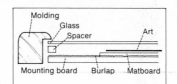

Rabbit crouches in a "pasture" of burlap ▶

The bright white of the rabbit featured in Toni Carner's silkscreen leaps to center stage against a quiet field of soft browns, doubly fenced—in the print and in the frame—by black. The rough texture of the burlap mat over which the work is mounted suits the wild spirit of the subject.

Black mat for balance

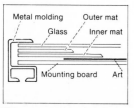

The power of a panther radiates from this pussycat as she exchanges challenging glances with a bluejay. Black was chosen for a mat that balances the cat's weight as it emphasizes her strength. Paler colors in the Dale de Armond woodcut might have receded inside a lighter or brighter mat.

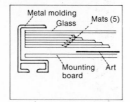

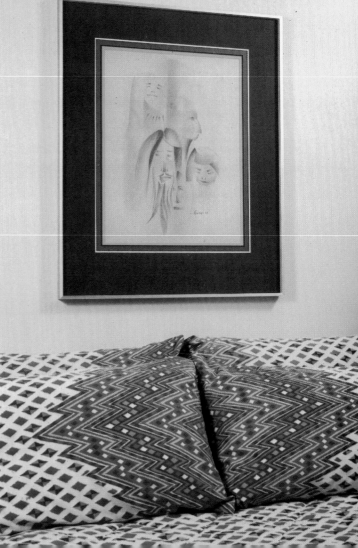

Blending picture tones with your room ▶

To relate Fernando Gomez's charcoal drawing to the batik bedspread and pillows below it, an earth-tone "rainbow" of mats was chosen. Each of the five tones repeats one of the batik dye colors. Yet the mats blend so smoothly that it's nearly impossible to see the colors separately.

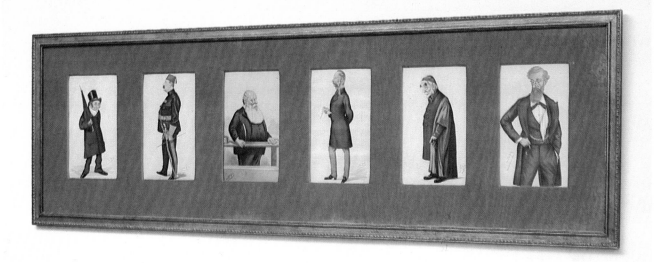

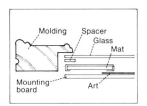

Each has his own niche

Once objects of a 19th century cartoonist's derision, six gentlemen from British public life retrieve some of their dignity today from a rich velvet mat that enshrines them individually. The windows were cut out of hardboard which was then covered with velvet.

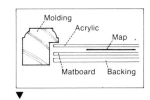

Tender treatment for antique chart

Handpainted and more than a century old, this navigational chart receives a full measure of the respect due antique treasures. Displayed out to its edges, it floats on a pale silk mat in a silver and gold-leafed frame.

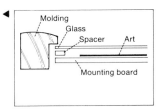

Powerful accent from suede

The deep burnt orange of a suede mat adds impact to the color of the persimmon celebrated by Toni Carner's serigraph scroll.

These frames focus on depth

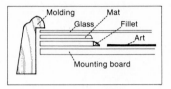

With an air of distinction ▶

Inside this elegant showcase of gold-leafed cap molding, windows cut in the silk-covered mat reveal a prized certificate and medal. Gold-leafed fillets outline the niches, giving each the appearance of a miniature frame.

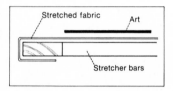

◀ Strength of canvas behind delicate paper

Canvas over stretcher bars provides a barely visible backbone for Charles Hilger's light and feathery paper sculpture. It allows the handmade paper to float loosely, casting crisp shadows.

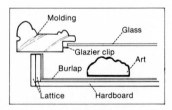

◀ Solemn gazes from antiquity

Shadow-boxed pre-Columbian clay sculptures stare back at you fearlessly as you study their primitive detail. Antiqued a rich burnt orange, the heavy molding-and-lattice shadow box seems to shelter the delicate figures, which are glued to the burlap lining. Directions for making a shadow-box appear on page 98. Design: Vicki Rutherford.

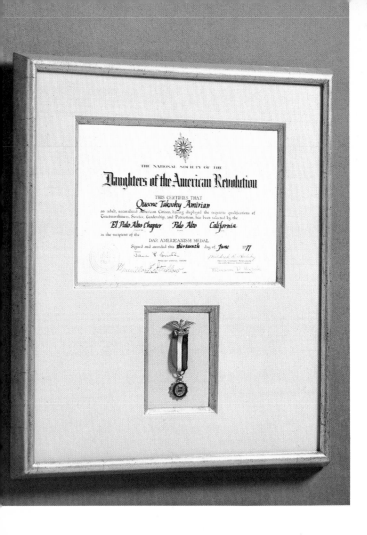

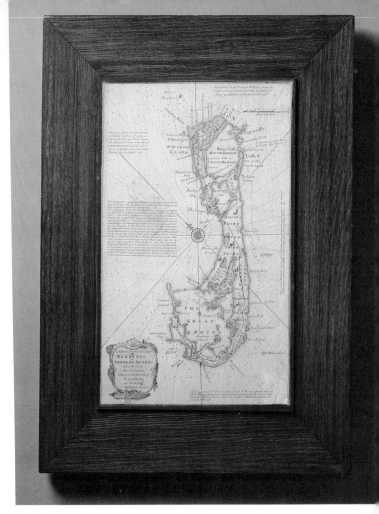

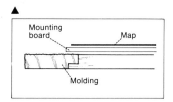

A platform for a frame

Aptly described as a "platform," this flat, rough-textured frame carries its subject in front of it. The antique map stands away from the frame by the 1/4-inch thickness of its mounting board.

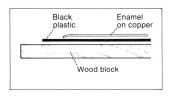

◄ Sophisticated look for the art of prehistory

Eons more sophisticated in a contemporary living room than their original cave wall counterparts, Margaret Roberts's "Indian petroglyphs" are mounted lack acrylic which is glued to a sturdy 8½ by 7-inch wooden block. Copied from actual incised rock carvings, the figures are depicted in enamel fired on copper.

Ways to treat oils & acrylics

◄ For miniatures, weighty frames

Three multiple-molding frames, each handsome and weighty yet quite different, emphasize the daintiness of these miniature oil paintings by Townsend Howe. At the same time, the cluster of frames helps to draw attention to the minute details inside them.

◄ Intensifying color

Subdued but warm in tone, a lustrous silk mat magically inflames the pale-to-vivid yellows in the painting—adding fire even to the accents of red. As a result, Sujarit's oil-on-canvas scene of Thai peasants in a rice paddy appears bathed in a soft golden glow.

The wall alone is frame enough

Unfettered by a frame, Dinah James's bold abstract—of mixed media on canvas—excites vivid sensations of freedom and strength. Even the most understated frame would appear to hem it in. Its stretcher bars hold the composition in relief from the wall—the only boundary needed.

Rose-glow against velvet

Exquisite, ornate, and traditional, this gold-leafed frame with red velvet liner and inner gold-leafed fillet sets off the glory of a perfect rose. Tani Boyle's oil painting captures the luster of the Sunset Jubilee rose, introduced to commemorate the 75th anniversary of *Sunset Magazine.*

◄ Traditional elegance for portrait display

Portraits in oil, even when rendered with the soft strokes of the Impressionists' mode, have a depth, weight, and richness that seem to call for ornate museum-style framing. This oil-on-wood painting by Edna Hibel is framed in heavy, deep gold-leafed molding and set off by a linen liner and gold-leafed fillet.

Photographs express your interests

Globetrotters' gallery board

For travelers weary of sorting through and projecting slides, this is an attractive alternative. Cluster prints of the best slides on a framed plywood mounting board. Here, the Aegean world sparkles on floater frames arranged against pale vinyl wallpaper that covers the plywood.
▼

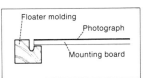

Floater molding
Photograph
Mounting board

Serene image, quiet treatment ▶
The misty, dreamlike tones of this wagon at rest in the snow evoke a contemplative mood. Setting the photograph out from the wall without the least distraction is the most understated of frames—a floater (characterized by the groove visible between the image and the molding edge).

NEIL LIEFER, ROBERT HUNTZINGER

Put some action on the wall ▶
Action bursts in flurries of sparkling snow from these poster-size prints—expressing a skier's love for the slopes. Photographs on the wall of favorite sports or hobbies start conversations and add a friendly personal touch to your room.

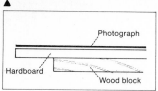

Exotic exhibit from slides
Dramatic and colorful prints unfold tales of Africa travel across this wood-paneled wall. Free of frames or mats, their striking formation has all the more impact. The mounted images, backed with wood blocks of varying thicknesses, overlap to create a three-dimensional effect.

...photographs

LEE ALLYN PARK   LEE ALLYN PARK

Open your room to a scenic "view"
An oversized scenic photograph, cut into "panes," creates the intriguing optical illusion of a window opening to a splendid view. Extruded aluminum frames separate the three sections.

24 PHOTOGRAPHS

▲
Open the family album
From great-great aunties to brand-new babies, photographs of the family no longer need to hide away in an album or bureau drawer. Photographic laboratories can make excellent copies (negatives aren't required), enlarging as necessary—so you can invite everyone to browse and reminisce through a family gallery.

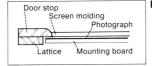

Door stop
Screen molding
Photograph
Lattice   Mounting board

▶

An ode to feline grace
See them purr, pose, stretch, nuzzle, and play—they almost look alive in this animated montage. Enjoy a candid camera show of children, pets, or the whole family by making a subdivided frame like this one. Directions appear on page 97.

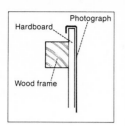

To keep your sights and ▶
spirits lofty

When you long to flee the hubbub but can't—here is a next-best-to-being-there gazing place on which to rest your eyes. The enlargement was wet mounted and wrapped around ¼-inch masonite. For wet-mounting information, see page 78. A frame of 1-inch strips, hidden at the back, holds the picture slightly away from the wall and prevents warping.

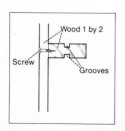

To show off prize photographs ▶

Five exciting scenes in striking formation compose a good-looking tribute to a photographer's skill in wind and spray. The grooved 1 by 2-inch rails, screwed together in a lattice, can display up to nine photographs.
Design: Drew Van Dis.

...photographs

If your enthusiasm is equestrian, ride with it
Infusing the room with spirit—and announcing an unabashed passion for horses—bold color prints are flush mounted to fit insert panels on wood cabinets.
▼

LEE ALLYN PARK

Poster power...
here's how to use it

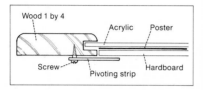

Wood 1 by 4 — Acrylic — Poster — Screw — Pivoting strip — Hardboard

For rotating poster display

This handsome oak frame, with its rounded corners and gently tapered sides, has a removable back to simplify changing its contents whenever you wish. Built with 1 by 4s, the frame has mitered corners reinforced with dowels. The poster is sandwiched between a sheet of clear acrylic and another of tempered hardboard. Short lengths of flat scrap metal, screwed to the frame, pivot to lock the hardboard in place. For building details, see page 95. Design: Tom Keller.

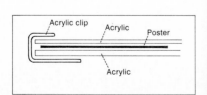

Acrylic clip — Acrylic — Poster — Acrylic

Art nouveau warms up a kitchen ▶

With its glowing tones of amber, gold, and gray green, this Mucha poster might have been commissioned especially for its cheerful surroundings. Its slim dimensions match it perfectly to the inside panel of a cupboard door. The poster is pressed between two sheets of clear acrylic which are held together by special clips.

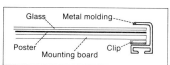

Poster gallery set off in silver
Nostalgia beguiles guests who are drawn to this grouping of travel posters and advertisements from the 1920s and '30s. A balance of contrasts in size and shape makes an appealing arrangement, and the uniformity of sleek, pencil-thin metal frames ties the group together.

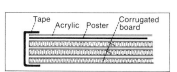

A tape trick ▶
Collect a few supplies from your local art or stationery store, and you can accomplish a trim, good-looking frame like this one—for very little cost. You'll need sheets of poster board, corrugated cardboard, and clear acetate film to fit the dimensions of your poster, and, for the frame itself, plastic-coated tape (available in several solid colors) about 1½ inches wide. Trim the poster board and cardboard to size; then snip the acetate film to fit over the poster. Lay the protected poster face-up over the cardboard, and carefully tape the layers together. (Don't use this method for valuable artwork, because the cardboard may cause discoloration after a few years.)

Frames for instant picture changes

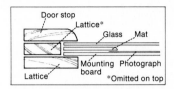

Art slips in or pulls out ▶

Hidden from view, a narrow slot in the top of this frame gives easy access when you want to exchange the spring wildflower for an autumn or winter scene. To make this frame, refer to information on page 96.

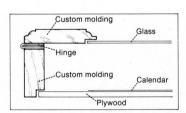

Novel, good-looking, ▶ and practical

Never in its wildest dreams would a humble kitchen calendar expect to reside in such a home. Designed like a shallow cabinet, the calendar frame has a door to open when the next month rolls along and you need to turn the page. The calendar hangs on a hook at the back of the cabinet.
Design: Roy Lipanovich.

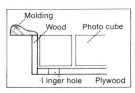

▲ Permanent "frame," removable art

These matted and mounted photographs slide into place between two strips of oval molding screwed permanently into the wall. If you like, a sheet of glass can be slipped over each picture at the same time. To recreate this system, choose either standard framing stock or the type of metal molding sold by building suppliers for attaching wall paneling.

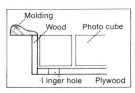

▲ Large and small—and more inside

If, like many fond and camera-happy parents, you have boxes, albums, and drawers spilling over with snapshots of your small darling—this frame of builder's moldings can help you out. Inside its depth sit four purchased acrylic cube frames. Each cube carries six photographs—so by shifting the cubes around, you can display up to 24 different views of your child (or children, or pets, or travels). You can even puzzle-piece together an enlargement, using all four cubes as we did.

Fabric as wall art...
here are possibilities

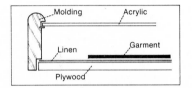

Spectacular splash of color . . . it's a _huipile_

Intensified by the simplicity of their surroundings, the colors in this handwoven _huipile_ fairly explode from the white mat, white frame, and white wall into the open, uncluttered room. Spread flat and tacked in place with careful stitches, the poncholike garment from Guatemala floats against its linen mat. Lightweight acrylic, rather than glass, fronts the frame.

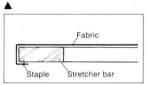

Fabric

Staple | Stretcher bar

As you turn the corner . . . a sunny surprise

Placed to greet you with its bold design and cheerful colors, this handsome fabric panel wakes up a short and otherwise forgettable wall. Directions appear on page 80 for pulling your own panel taut on artists' stretcher bars. Today's graphic fabrics, printed with dramatic, grand-scale motifs, are often designed specifically to become fabric "paintings." But browse before you choose: any number of prints intended for sewing could look just as stunning on the wall.

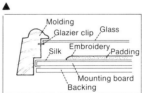

Molding
Glazier clip / Glass
Silk / Embroidery / Padding
Mounting board
Backing

Elegant display for Chinese embroidery

Rich brown silk and gilded cap-on-stem molding set off the warm tones and ornate detail of this embroidery from China. The piece was stitched to a circle of ragboard, which was then glued to the silk lining of the shallow, glass-faced shadowbox.

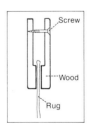

Screw

Wood

Rug

◄ Safe, attractive mounting for valuable rugs

More open to view and safer from soil than it would be underfoot, this exquisite Navajo rug also warms up the adobe wall on which it is mounted. Tightly sandwiched between two strips of pine that attach it to the wall without penetrating its weave, the rug can easily be removed.

. . . fabrics

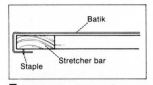
Batik — Stretcher bar — Staple

Batik bathed in natural light
A skylight directly overhead washes over the natural dyes used by Sri Lanka artist Enid da Silva in this elephant-theme batik. The fabric art is pulled smooth on stretcher bars (see page 80 for how to fashion such a panel yourself). A border worked into the intricate design gives the batik a framed appearance.

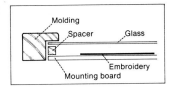

◀ Stately display for Imperial splendor

Gleaming against a raw silk mat, this antique Chinese embroidery holds stately court in its formal gold-leafed frame. The surrounding blue wall—and blue detail in the Imari plate displayed below—intensify the luster of the predominant silk threads in the fabric.

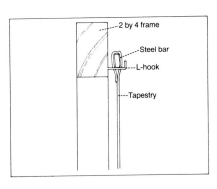

◀ Tapestry hangs free, like a banner

A strip of sturdy steel, slipped through the upper hem of this abstract Borisov tapestry, rests in L-hooks placed near the edges of an austere frame of 2 by 4s. Painted black for emphatic contrast, the frame creates a fine delineation between the yellow background of the tapestry and the white wall surrounding it.

Crafts & folk art dress up these walls

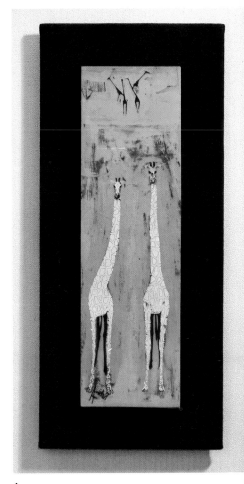

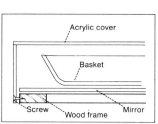

Mirror reveals hidden dimensions

An African basket appears almost to float against the wall in its transparent acrylic box. The mirror against which the basket is glued offers a bonus view of the side that would otherwise never be seen. Design: Karl Mann Associates.

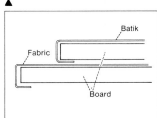

A stately vertical

A strong vertical display for this pair of giraffes accentuates their lofty grace. The batik is stretched on a $\frac{1}{2}$-inch-thick block which is screwed to a second block $\frac{1}{2}$ inch thick and felt-covered.

◄ Cool color on the wall

Falling free and loose, Enola Dickey's weaving, done in subtly rippling blues and greens, makes an appealingly casual wall decoration. Integral to the total design, brass curtain rods woven across the warp yarns and ceramic medallions linked to the lower edge also serve to keep the weaving straight.

...crafts & folk art

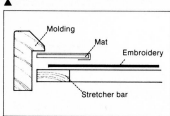

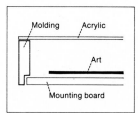

▲ **Elegant shadow box for primitive art**
Lined in natural linen, a shallow shadow box with acrylic cover harmonizes with the soft buff tones in this feather collage. Design: Karl Mann Associates.

Vibrant colors sing out
The colors chosen for this austere, flat wood frame and linen mat bring out the brilliance of a Peruvian yarn embroidery. Rich purple, surrounding the stitchery, complements its quieter tones while making the most of its pinks and reds. The bronzy metallic finish applied to the frame accentuates the yellow and orange motifs—without competing.

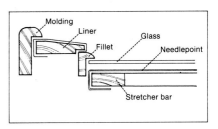

◄ Regal colors, rich textures

The combination of ornate half-round molding, a velvet liner, and gold-leafed fillet suits the formality of this needlepoint tapestry. First blocked and stretched, the work was then covered with nonglare glass. The glass protects the tapestry while softening its stitches just enough to give it the look of an oil painting.

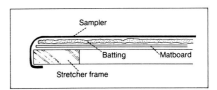

◄ An American folk classic: sentiment captured in cross-stitch

Reminiscent of long ago, a lovingly worked sampler is fittingly treated in multicurved oak molding. The stitchery was backed by a thin layer of polyester batting over matboard, then pulled over a stretcher frame. To keep the slightly cushioned look, the owner chose not to use glass.

Fanciful frames...
easy, fun, good-looking

Lush, upholstered look ▶
Lightly poufed fabric in sprightly prints make a soft and pretty surrounding for mirrors and family photographs. Create your own luxuriant fabric-covered frame and mat, following the directions on page 92.

◀ She peeks through a ribbon frame
Looking lavishly embroidered, this purchased frame is actually covered with fancy ribbon. For each side, cut a piece of ribbon long enough to wrap around both ends. Lightly sand the frame; then paint it with white glue, allowing the glue to thicken slightly before smoothing the ribbon in place.

◀ Striking mosaic mirror
Sunflower seeds and black-eyed peas take on an elegant feathered look when glued to a flat wood frame in a simple mosaic. For a different effect, any number of small variegated objects (beads or seashells, for example) could be substituted. Sand the frame lightly and sketch a pattern to follow on its surface. Use white glue that is slightly tacky, pushing the objects in place with a toothpick.

▲ Paint around a portrait

Design your own unique and colorful glass frame for the annual school portrait—or show your child the simple technique. First, sketch your design on paper, outlining a central opening to keep clear for the photograph (trace children's book illustrations or stitchery patterns if you feel unsure of drawing freehand). Lay the glass over the drawing. Using acrylic paints, fill in the design on the back of the glass, starting with surface details and finishing with the background. Let each color dry completely before applying the next. To finish, slip the portrait behind the opening, cover the back with heavy paper, and tape paper and glass together with plastic-coated tape.

◀ Like home movies . . . photo strips

These good-looking strip frames house a series of camera glimpses of each child in the family. The multiple portrait effect is fascinating—fun to study for kids, parents, and visitors alike. Overlaying the photographs, and fixing them to wood blocks, are perforated strips of metal salvaged from a machine shop. After screw holes were drilled and corners rounded, they were painted to mesh attractively as a wall grouping. Design: Darrow M. Watt.

Show off & share
a prized collection

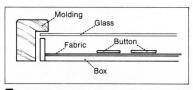

A bounty of buttons

This neatly boxed assembly of antique buttons calls to mind the trim display cases of an old-fashioned dry goods store. Sorted by size, colors, and style, the buttons are stitched to lightly padded velvet and encased under glass in shallow wood shadowboxes. Design: Elizabeth Poot.

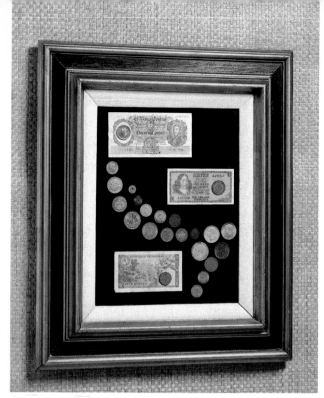

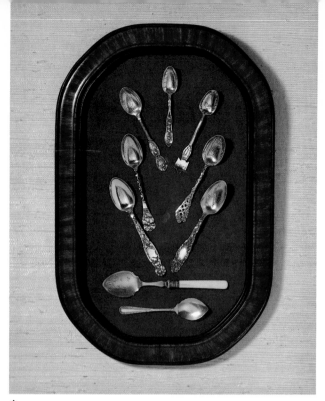

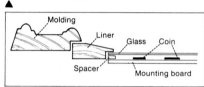

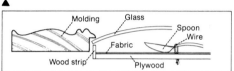

If you can't spend it, frame it

Many travelers bring home a cache of fascinating—and often quite beautiful—coins and paper bills from the countries they visit. Here currency from various corners of the world is arranged under glass. Glued to velvet and given a linen liner, the collage is set off in a decorative combination frame. Design: Judith A. Gaulke.

Silver splendor under glass

A formal display of antique spoons, arranged under convex glass in an elegantly curved Victorian frame, stands out against a background of green velvet. Design: Vicki Rutherford.

Clean mounting for sharp focus ▶

Without the interference that even the narrowest frame would cause, the eye travels immediately to the fine sculptural detail of these pre-Columbian clay figures. The 36-inch acrylic circle on which they are fixed with silicone rubber cement reflects delicate shadow patterns. A hole, cut in the circle for hanging, is hidden by the top figure. Design: Christina Lockwood.

...collections

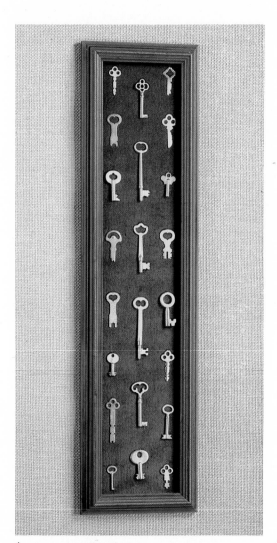

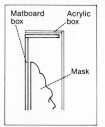

Matboard box — Acrylic box

Mask

Their beauty is striking, their fierce looks startling

Arranged in a wheel of fiery color in a matboard box, miniatures of Nepalese ceremonial masks strike an emphatic chord against their subdued background. A nearly invisible 1¼-inch-deep acrylic shadow box protects the brilliantly lacquered faces, which are glued to the matboard. Design: Jane Hastings.

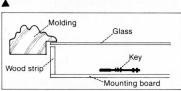

Molding — Glass — Key
Wood strip — Mounting board

Keys on corduroy

A textured background of corduroy enhances the metallic sheen of these keys and provides good contrast behind their ornamental silhouettes. After their positions were marked on the back of the poster board to which the corduroy is glued, the keys were tacked in place with beige thread. The elongated proportions of their shallow shadow box harmonize with the strong vertical shapes in the collection. Design: Jini Johnson.

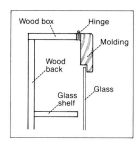

Eskimo carvings invite a close look
Miniatures of Alaskan wildlife parade along glass shelves inside a simple 5 by 20 by 1-inch black shadow box. A background of marbleized paper (traditionally used in bookbinding but more accessible today as wallpaper) provides sharp contrast for the delicate ivory carvings. Design: Jane Hastings.
▼

◀ **Clockwork collages in a cluster**
A collection of dismantled watches, each with its regalia of shiny bits and pieces, invites close inspection. Each clockwork collage is glued to a velvet backing and housed in an ornate shadow box. Design: Marylee Meadows.

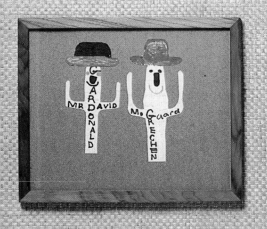

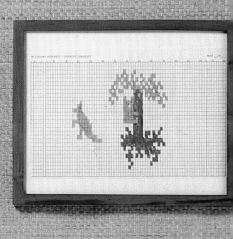

Young artists deserve attention

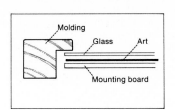

Molding

Glass Art

Mounting board

▲
Memorable works treasured in teak
The three artists whose works are shown here have since grown up—but their parents still enjoy comparing each child's personality with its expression on paper earlier in life. The trio of favorites from the past is handsomely treated in simple, glass-faced teak frames.

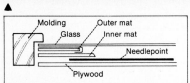

▲
Molding Outer mat
Glass Inner mat
Needlepoint
Plywood

Canine hero immortalized
Looking pleased by the honor bestowed through hours of stitching by a 13-year-old, this cartoon hero grants his needleworking fan a woolly grin. The 3½- by 4-inch canvas was blocked, then stretched over thin plywood. A white burlap mat repeats the nubby texture of the stitches.

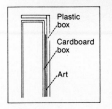

Plastic box

Cardboard box

Art

▲
Bright and beautiful . . . from a three-year-old
A small girl's splashy paintings sing out with a zesty spirit that would be hard to match by anyone more mature. Boldly displayed against burlap, each painting is mounted at the front of a clear acrylic box over mat paper chosen to amplify the artist's cheerful palette.

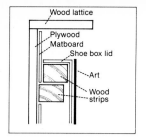

◀ To display any number of pictures

Children are often such prolific artists that to display everything they draw or paint requires ingenuity. One solution is to set up a revolving art show in this versatile frame. The happy scene shown here is wrapped around a removable shoe box lid. The lid hangs on a horizontal strip of wood that juts through a slot in the mat from the back of the outer frame. You just lift it off when you want to change pictures. For more on how to make this frame, refer to page 101. Design: John Matthias.

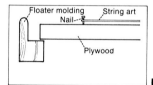

Eye-catching abstract wakes up the wall

The family was impressed when their ten-year-old created this geometric maze of string. But the electric colors in his design really came to life when the artwork was mounted on the wall, projecting from a metal-faced, 9-inch-square floater frame.

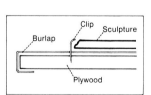

◀ Clay sculpture invites both looking and touching

Handsome against earthy red burlap, the terrain of this second-grader's sculpture tempts you to probe its rises, hollows, and varied textures. Metal clips secure it to the covered board behind it.

FRAMING YOUR PICTURE

As the interest in art has escalated in recent years, so has the desire to hang something on our walls. Original art, reproductions, prints of various kinds, photographs, crafts, and all sorts of collections are among the things we display on our walls. And with these trends have come greater appreciation and demand for good framing.

Tastes in framing change as do tastes in art, clothing, and just about everything else in our lives. After World War II, New York's Museum of Modern Art began displaying paintings in narrow strip frames, and soon the rest of us started framing everything in narrow, plain moldings of wood and metal. Now that trend is reversing toward richer and more decorative framing, closely following the trend in interior design toward lusher and more opulent decor.

Because framing designs are not static, there are no absolutes and no firm rules for us to follow. The so-called rules of one period often seem in bad taste to later generations. As a result, selecting attractive framing can be a difficult task for most of us.

If you are one of that majority, read on. In the pages that follow, you'll discover the reasons for framing and the functions of the various components; you'll learn how to select the appropriate framing components to fill your need; you'll even find out how to cut mats, make frames, put everything together, and arrange the results on a wall.

Reasons for framing

Whatever your motivation for framing a picture, it will fit one or more of three broad categories: esthetics, protection, and support.

Esthetics. Framing focuses and limits the eye to the pictures, reinforces the more elusive elements and color tones, increases the size of the piece, and serves as a transition between the picture and the wall on which it hangs.

For you as the owner of a piece of art—be it an oil, watercolor, print, photograph, whatever—the esthetics of framing may have different dimensions. You may intend to use the framed picture as part of a room's decor, display it for its own sake as art, or just enjoy it as part of your daily life.

Protection. Simply keeping the picture free from dust and grime is the protection most of us expect from framing. However another, more specialized, type of protection—conservation framing—is of great interest to museums and other serious collectors of art and should be of interest to you if you own valuable or potentially valuable art. Conservation framing (see page 72) protects the art not only from outside contaminants but also from damage by the framing materials themselves.

Support. Framing supports the art in the proper position for viewing, usually flat and vertical. The frame itself contains the art and other framing components: glass, mats, and backings.

Options for framing

Having decided that a picture is to be framed, you must decide how best to accomplish the task. Your options depend on your esthetic goals, your skills, your pocketbook, and the time available to you. A busy schedule might lead you to choose a custom framer. On the other hand, if you must have that certain picture framed and on your dining room wall for your guests to admire next weekend, the only option may be to do the work yourself.

There are other reasons for selecting a custom framer as you will read below. If you elect to do all or part of the job yourself, you can choose between several available alternatives.

The custom framer

With the possible exception of those who use ready-made frames, most people employ the services of custom framers. Though this usually is the more expensive approach, it has some definite advantages.

The experienced custom framer shares with you a wealth of expertise gained over a period of years while framing hundreds and thousands of pieces of art. Not only the framer's craftsmanship, but his or her knowledge of art and of color, shape, and proportion assure you of a framed picture that you will enjoy owning.

If you own fine art or pieces that are potentially valuable (presumably, almost any original art has the potential for becoming valuable) you'll want to select a framer experienced in conservation framing (page 72). With this technique, acid-free materials and proper assembly methods are employed to protect the art from discoloration, dirt, and insects. Conservation framing techniques do add to the cost and are not warranted in many framing situations.

As with most types of businesses, the quality of work and design varies among custom framers, and so do prices. The different framings of Dürer's *Young Field Hare* shown on pages 10 and 11 demonstrate that there are many right ways to frame a work of art. The costs varied widely because of the different materials and labor costs. Since it's unlikely that any two framers will offer you exactly the same framing design, evaluating prices is quite difficult. The best rule may be this: if you are satisfied with your art after it is framed, then the price is fair.

Recommendations of friends and—in the case of valuable art—museum curators can be helpful. If you see a frame that impresses you in a friend's home or a place of business, find out who did the work. Most framers, particularly if they are proud of their work, place a label on the back.

Doing your own thing

If you elect to frame your own picture, you have several alternatives to choose from, and you may be able to mix and match—do the whole job or any part that you wish.

Do-it-yourself framing shops. The increasing trend of people to do things for themselves, both for pleasure and for economy, is reflected in the picture framing industry. In many metropolitan and suburban areas, you can find frame shops that cater to the do-it-yourselfer; many provide custom framing services as well, to utilize fully the staff and facilities. Some of the specialized knowledge of a custom framer may be missing from these establishments, though.

For most people, the best choice is the shop that has a large selection of moldings and mat materials, offers design help, and provides professional facilities and instruction so you can do the whole job. Because of safety considerations, staff members usually cut the molding and glass on professional equipment, and some may cut the mat.

In another type of shop, staff members provide design assistance and supplies, cut all the materials, and send you home to put everything together. Unless you have the proper tools (see page 63), you may run into problems.

Because the amount of work done by the shop varies, so does the cost saving. Still, you may save 10 to 30 percent compared to custom framing, and you can brag to family and friends about your accomplishment.

Lumberyards. Some lumberyards, particularly those catering to homeowners, have framing departments. You will find worktables, miter boxes, and saws, clamps, and the other tools needed to make a frame, but you'll have to go elsewhere for mats, glass, and other materials needed to complete the job. Most give instruction if requested, but the choice of molding is up to you and may be limited to a small selection of finished and unfinished moldings. Molding quality varies, so select carefully.

Framing at home. If you have the inclination and skill, framing at home in your own shop can save money and give pleasure. There are some problems, though.

The cost of the basic tools (see page 63) can be significant, but if you choose picture framing as a hobby, the cost will be justified. You may have trouble buying the right molding. Many frame shops will not sell lengths of molding ("sticks," in the trade) to do-it-yourselfers. There are mail-order sources, and most will sell you a set of samples, but styles are often limited and quality may be uncertain.

Some people enjoy making and finishing their own moldings. You can design a molding by combining two or three builder's moldings (the kind used to trim houses—see page 94). If you are a woodworker, you can make your own moldings with a table or radial-arm saw, router, shaper, or even a molding plane. The cost saving is substantial and so is the pleasure.

Ready-made frames. For many, the solution to a framing problem lies in a ready-made frame. Most of us are familiar with the simple wood, metal, and plastic frames found in variety and other stores. Also available from ready-made frame shops and some art supply stores are more ornate and decorated frames in standard sizes. Take a look and you may find a frame that suits your taste and fits your picture. If you need a mat, you'll find some ready-mades are available, or you can buy it from one of the other sources mentioned in the preceding paragraphs. Design help varies—you may be on your own. However, good results are possible and you can save money. See the special feature on page 59 for additional ideas.

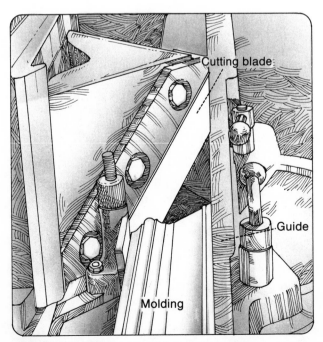

Molding cutter, called "chopper," is used by many professional framers to miter picture moldings.

Good Framing Begins with Good Design

Whatever the subject, it's almost always easy to make decisions when your choices are limited, much harder when they're not. But framing is an exception —today, frame design choices are unlimited, yet your chances of making the right decision are excellent. Because rigid rules are suspended, we look for guidelines. The information that follows contains such design guidelines.

The flexibility of good design

Professional designers view this time as the best of times—one in which we are not locked into a single, oppressive conformity. Look about you as you walk along the busy streets of our cities, or through the shopping malls, or the plazas of contemporary buildings. Do all the women dress the same as did, say, the flappers of the Roaring Twenties? And how about the men? Are they less well dressed if they opt for well-tailored sports outfits rather than three-piece suits?

Or visit a friend's home. Does the living room feature a three-piece "suite" of identically styled sofa and chairs, each piece upholstered with fabric from the same bolt? Are the pictures on the wall all of one era or one medium? Do their frames match each other slavishly?

The answer to all of these loaded questions is an obvious no. Today's professional designers compromise, adapt, and harmonize. Yet, with all their new freedoms, they produce results that never look haphazard or unplanned.

You as a designer

How do you plug professional designers' concepts into your own work? As a first step, consider a basic principle of design, one that has bailed out many a pro challenged with the request to "use your judgment, but keep it in good taste." The principle is "Form ever follows function." It's a sound one, its validity demonstrated in the work left by its originator, Louis Sullivan, designer of some of our first skyscrapers. Many of them still stand as reminders of gentleness, intellect, and wit in design.

What, then, are the functions of picture framing? Simply these:
• It must glorify, celebrate, and enhance the picture —not compete with it.
• It must establish limits so that the room environment doesn't impinge on the picture, nor the picture on its environment.
• It must serve as a transition between wall and picture.
• It must protect the artwork.

When framing performs its functions well, it makes pleasing esthetic contributions—first, to its picture; second, to its room.

The framing and the picture. The right framing enhances its picture by sensitizing the viewer to its composition, by bringing alive the picture's some-

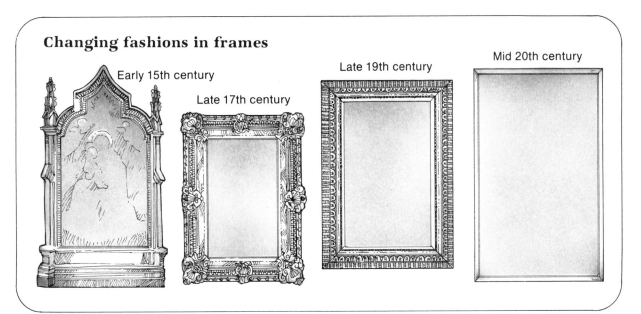

Changing fashions in frames

Early 15th century

Late 17th century

Late 19th century

Mid 20th century

Sumptuous to simple: Frame from early 15th century is extension of architectural components. Typical of late 17th century is the richly decorated and gilded frame. Late 19th century Victorians favored mixture of decoration. Austere stick frames were in vogue in the 1950s.

times transitory color touches and linear elements, and by giving proportion to the picture.

And the wrong framing? History holds examples of frames that did violence to their artworks. Many great paintings of the Victorian era, for example, were originally surrounded by framing that overwhelmed them, diminishing their artistic impact. Their true worth couldn't be recognized until someone who applied principles of good design reframed them in simpler moldings and inserts.

Framings that cramp pictures—that is, fail to allow breathing space between the molding and the artwork by use of a mat or a liner—also do violence to the subject. Many a simple, unimpressive picture has been given special character when crowding was corrected. But this admonition isn't hard and fast. Framing that is of the same color as the picture doesn't cramp it—doesn't stop its visual flow. Subtly, simply, it serves as a trim to the finished edge and can work quite well.

A frame that is too narrow, particularly if it's bright in color, can stifle a rich subject. Often a frame that uses a molding that *suggests* the period in which the artwork was created, will enhance the picture, while a costly antique frame that is actually of the period can, if it is too ornamental, draw the eye away from the art and cancel its artistic integrity.

Rustic scenes call for rustic framings. To mount a watercolor of a weathered barn on a California coast in a gilded frame lined with a starkly colored mat is not good design. Neither is a portrait of a Flemish noble if mounted, say, in a driftwood frame.

Yet it is possible, even good design sometimes, to mount a work of one period into the framing of another. If a Picasso drawing looks good in a simple, late-19th century American frame, then it should be in that frame.

The framing and the room. Freedom in design does not mean chaos. But with the new freedoms, you *can* place a functionally modern steel-and-smoked-acrylic reading lamp in a room that is predominantly 18th century French neo-Classic; you *can* put a treasured antique table in a room that is mainly contemporary; and you *can* hang a modern painting in a room of just about any period. The framing will serve as the transition. Let's imagine an example:

You are the proud owner of an original abstract painting and you want to display it directly over a fireplace rich in neo-Classic decoration. Even though the painting is modern, it could be housed in a framing that suggests an 18th century look, in keeping with the surroundings. Just be sure to separate the 20th century work from its 18th-century-style frame by a modest liner, preferably one of neutral color.

Let's take the painting to another setting—a study with a book-lined wall and a trestle table for a desk. The unadorned molding of the double frame and the linen-covered mat allow the painting to blend harmoniously with the simplicity of the room.

If you were to hang that modern painting in a room where the motif is early American, you'd have to choose other framing to bridge the differences between the decor and the painting. Try an ogee or swan molding for this transition—even a colonial-type molding. In any case, use a liner so that the frame does not dilute the strength of the painting.

Plain, light-colored walls make the best background on which to display framed art. The more decorative the wall finish, the more difficult it becomes to display the framed art to the best advantage. If the only wall available is busily papered or covered with fabric, make sure the frame elements isolate the subject much more than if the wall were plain.

Frame without mat appears to cramp Dürer's Young Owl. *Addition of a double mat allows breathing space while still containing the subject.*

Abstract painting, *separated from its partially ornate period frame by a modest liner, is at home in 18th century decor.*

Same abstract *in angular double frame fits into the austere decor of this study.*

Colonial-style molding *bridges gap between the 20th century abstract and an early American room.*

Color in framing design

Whether they are working in oils, acrylics, gouaches, watercolors, pastels, serigraphs (silkscreens), or any other color medium, artists are ever sensitive to concerns about color. They expend prodigious amounts of creative energy to get exactly what they want in colors, even though their results may seem easy and casual.

The language of color

Color in paintings and other forms of visual art is light reflected from their surfaces. Similarly, the colors we perceive on grass, in trees and flowers, in clothing, buildings, cars—in *most* of the world about us—is reflected light. Most? Yes, most. Color on your TV screen is projected, not reflected. Anyway, it's already framed.

The source of reflected color is celestial: the pure white light of the sun, which contains all the colors in the spectrum. Though that purity is modified a bit by the atmosphere, it's a healthy, usable white. White is the total of all colors, a truth demonstrated when a shaft of light passes through a prism. Emerging from the adjacent side is the *color spectrum.* The color with the longest wavelength is red, the warmest color. As the wavelengths shorten, the colors become cooler. Naming but six of the infinite number of spectral variations, the progression ranges from red through orange, through yellow, green, and blue, up to purple.

Primary colors. Three of the colors listed—red, yellow, and blue—are called the primary colors because you can't create them by blending other colors.

Secondary colors. When you mix two primary colors in equal amounts you create a secondary color. For starters, blend red and yellow and you come up with the color of a ripe orange. Mix that same red with the other primary, blue, and the result is a delicious purple, close to that of an eggplant. Want a pure green? Then combine blue and yellow.

The intermediate colors. There are six of these and they also result from blending of primaries. Mix more red than blue in your recipe and you come up with magenta. Reverse that balance—use more blue than red—and you can revel in another intermediate, blue purple. Vary blends of red and yellow for versions of orange, then mix blue with yellow in similar fashion, and you'll have come full circle, like the revolution of a wheel.

The color wheel. Add all the primaries, secondaries, and intermediates and you'll come up with 12 main colors, called *hues.* Hues are the building blocks of all conceivable colors, and they are traditionally arrayed as a color wheel (see drawing on next page).

The color wheel circulates from light colors to dark and then to light again. Colors that fall opposite each other on the wheel are *complementary*—yellow is

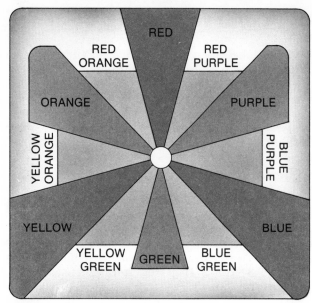

Color wheel *shows relationship between hues, made up of primary, secondary, and intermediate colors.*

names. Common names, such as rose or pink, describe tints of red; then there are powder blue and lavender—one a tint of blue, the other of purple. Tints emerge as less bold than their parent hues. Most of the colors called "pastels" are tints.

But suppose you want to increase the boldness and strength of a hue? Add black and you get a *shade*. Maroon is a shade of red, midnight blue a shade of blue.

If a hue is too intense, too warm, or too cold, and you want to dull it, add gray—a combination of black and white—to the hue. The result is a *tone*.

Using neutral colors. Brilliantly colored, even subtly colored art can sometimes be advantageously displayed within framing elements of *neutral* colors. What are the neutrals? Black, white, and gray in one group; the "earth colors"—tan, beige, ecru, ivory, cream, and their variations—in another.

Black, white, and gray don't appear on color wheels and can't be created from colors on the wheels. But while they aren't colors as viewed through scientific eyes, we've all been conditioned to call them colors, and it is practical to do so.

Some ways to use color in framing

Knowing the solar genesis of colors, the physics of the color spectrum, and the nomenclature is stimulating and intellectually rewarding, like knowing the precision innards of a sports car or the intricacies of a finely wrought camera. But when you downshift that car on a hairpin turn, or point that lens at an ocean sunset, you don't give much thought to the mechanics of the machine you are controlling.

Similarly, framing is not a laboratory procedure, though the roots of color's origins lie deep in science. Framing is a craft, a hobby, even an *art*. Your knowl-

(Continued on page 56)

complementary to purple, red to green, blue to orange.

Those that lie next to each other are *related* colors. Yellow orange is related to yellow on one side and orange on the other.

Tints, shades, and tones. These terms classify the infinite variations of the 12 hues. Remember that when a surface reflects all the colors in the spectrum and absorbs none, the result is white. Black surfaces, though, absorb all the colors and reflect none. Technically, black is the absence of color. Black and white are catalysts in forming the endless variety of colors based on the 12 hues. Add some white to a hue and you have a *tint*. Tints bear an astronomical variety of

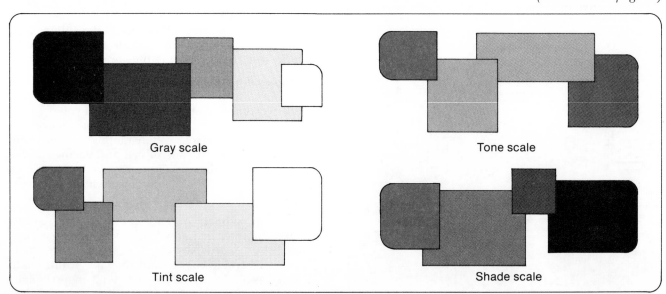

Color scales *show variations of hues. Make tints by adding white to hues, shades by adding black, tones by adding gray (a mixture of white and black).*

What's what in framing

Before going into the design and mechanics of framing, you need to be familiar with the purpose and function of the various framing components.

Backing. Additional pieces of matboard or other types of cardboard placed behind the mounting board to provide additional rigidity and support to the art.

Dust seals. These keep dirt, grime, and insects from getting into the framed art and damaging or discoloring it. The usual dust seal is a sheet of heavy paper stretched across the back of the frame and glued to the back of the molding. Another dust seal, a strip of tape, is sometimes applied to the joint between the glass and the molding (on the back side of the frame).

Fillet. See Liner.

Frame. This is the structure that supports and contains the picture and all the other framing elements. There are several types of frames: wood, metal, plastic, cardboard, novelty, stretcher, and various kinds of frames so inconspicuous that they could be called "nonframes" (see page 59). As commonly used, the word "frame" also means all the assembled components of the finished product.

Glass. Transparent material covers most types of framed art to protect the surface. Plastic sheet is sometimes used instead of glass, but there are problems with this material (see page 87). To reduce reflection, nonreflecting types of glass and plastic have been developed. However, they tend to dull colors and they may impart a fuzzy appearance, especially if the art is separated from the glass. Except in the case of old or delicate paintings, glass is not used with oils or acrylics because the artist finishes such work with a transparent protective coating.

Hangers. This is the hardware attached to the back of the framed art and to the wall to hold the art in position for display.

Liner. A liner is a flat molding, sometimes beveled, that fits between the art and the frame. Usually liners are used with oil paintings and serve the same visual purpose as a mat. Though most liners are covered with fabric, gold leaf may be used for finish, as may gold, silver, or colored paint. Sometimes a narrow molded liner, also known as a fillet, is placed between a fabric-covered liner and the art. This may be a separate molding or integral with the liner. The fillet is most often finished in gold or silver but may be colored.

Mat. A mat is a flat piece of cardboard, wood, or other material that provides a transition from the art to the frame, serving to focus the eyes on the art. When the picture is covered with glass, the mat separates the art from the glass; without this separation or airspace between the art and the glass, moisture, mold, fungus, or ink transfer might damage the art. More than one mat may be used with a picture. Mats may be plain, decorated, or covered with fabric, foil, gold leaf, or other material.

Molding. The basic element from which a frame is constructed, moldings are most often made of wood; some are available in metal or plastic, or in combinations. There are thousands of molding designs available, but they can all be classified into five basic shapes: flat, angular, curved, multiple-curved, and compound (a combination of curves and angles).

Mounting board. This is a piece of matboard that holds the art firmly against the mat. The art may be attached to the mounting board with paper hinges or, in some cases, may be glued to the mounting board. (See "Mounting your art," beginning on page 77.)

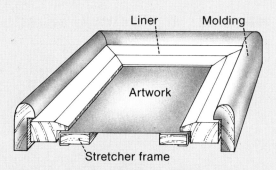

Framing components for canvas artwork.

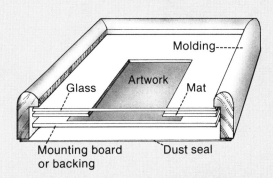

Framing parts for paper artwork.

. . . Continued from page 54

edge of color science will aid your use of color in framing, but unlike the science of color, the *art of color* doesn't have to be the slave of immutable laws. Like the artist, the framer can allow imagination and creativity to soar. Here are some suggestions, not rules, on how you can use color in framing design.

The picture itself. You may wish to "pick up" one of the hues, tints, shades, or tones in the work you are about to frame. Should you try to *match* that color in a mat, liner, or frame? Give it a go, but know that if the match is not perfect it will stand out like a sore thumb. Perhaps you ought to try a complementary, related, or *dissonant* color—that is, a hue, shade, tone, or tint that lies somewhere on the color wheel *between* a complementary and related color. Any of the options will work—will pick up that color. The choice is yours. And if it is emotionally satisfying, it is a valid choice.

Colors from the wall, the decor. These factors are "external influences," as contrasted with "internal influences"—that is, those framing color choices the picture itself offers. The effect of external influences is considerably less than that of the picture colors when you choose framing colors, and if wall and decor colors are neutral or light, their effect is minimal. Of the two, the wall color exerts more influence than the colors used in decor.

If the picture is one that you or your interior designer selected to enhance the decor, then the framing should also enhance the decor. But if you selected the picture to display as a piece of art, you must isolate it from its surroundings. This is particularly true if you intend to hang it on a wall finished in a strong color or a busy wallpaper. The isolation of such an artwork usually is accomplished by the shape and finish of the molding (see page 60).

The framing can change the picture's colors. Color is affected by its surroundings, as illustrated below. This phenomenon is a demonstration of *chromatic adaptation,* the tendency of the human eye to lose its sensitivity to the color of an object and

to become more sensitive to the color of its surroundings.

Therefore, if framers, instead of picking up colors in pictures, want or need merely to modify the impact of the colors, they can do so by choosing from among a variety of mat or liner colors. But other colors in the picture will be affected, tco. The molding? Unless it's in direct contact with the art, as it is in oils and acrylics, it won't have a *strong* color-changing effect, but it will cast its influence.

Bold colors and pale colors. Yet another optical adaptation happens in relation to the strength or weakness of a color. A heavily saturated, intense color—wherever it lies in the warm-to-cool spectrum—when centered on a pale background, will seem to be closer to the viewer than its background. It "advances." Conversely, a pale color, even one that derives from a hue as warm as red, will appear to be farther from the viewer than its more intense background. It "recedes." Framers make use of this phenomenon when selecting mat colors. A mat in a soft tint will not overpower the soft tones of a pastel and will accentuate the strong colors of a gouache.

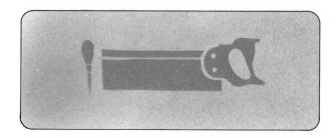

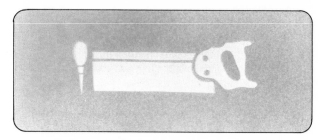

Colors more intense than background seem closer to viewer; those lighter than background appear to recede.

Surrounded by black, *colors appear darker than when they enclose black.*

Avenues to tasteful framing

We can indulge in fantasies about homes perched on eminences facing crashing surfs, but most of us live in simpler abodes. Likewise, few of us will acquire great original art, but modestly priced originals abound at art fairs and galleries. You may even have done your own and want to display them. Hanging good prints of great originals is also a source of pleasure. Whatever the medium, tastefully framed pictures help to establish a hospitable environment in a home.

There are many "correct" ways to frame and as

Three approaches to matting a black and white photograph using only black and gray mats. Pewter-finished frame in last photograph works with each matted picture.

many "incorrect" ways. When friends fail to notice a picture you cherish, it may be a clue that the frame is "incorrect," but there just aren't any sharply defined rights and wrongs. If a frame serves the functions noted on page 51 of this section, chances are it's in good taste and will cause visitors to gravitate toward the picture it celebrates. The following examples are offered as clues to tasteful framing.

Some traditions of framing

Though we are no longer constrained by rigid guidelines in the selection of our framing, sound esthetic and practical considerations have developed into certain framing standards that have been proven by time. Let's take a look at these traditional treatments for various categories of artistic mediums.

Graphics. On line drawings, lithographs, silkscreens, and etchings, use narrow moldings with wide, off-white mats. Some contemporary graphics, done in bold colors and patterns, require strong frames.

The window in the mat should be large enough to show the plate mark and signature, and the mat itself should be large enough to cover the art untrimmed. Glass or acrylic is required for protection. The mat separates the art from the glass, preventing moisture damage, mold and fungus growth, and ink transfer from the art to the glass.

Watercolors. Some of the world's most treasured paintings are done in this gentle medium. Delicate frames made from small moldings—flat, half-round, and ogee—are suggested. Combine them with medium to wide mats (3 to 5 inches) in colors that won't overpower the work. Watercolors tend naturally to warp and buckle, and this is not a sign of inferiority. Easily damaged by waterspotting, they must be kept scrupulously dry. Glass and a mat in front, and a good dust cover behind will minimize this danger.

Gouaches. These are also painted with water paints, but the colors are strong and often undiluted. The vivid, opaque medium calls for a heavier frame than

the one you choose for a watercolor. Glass and matting normally are required. Some techniques of gouache give effects similar to oils, and framing should also be similar.

Pastels and charcoal and pencil drawings. The light treatment of these mediums calls for frames as delicate as for watercolors. Surface protection is needed, for these mediums smear easily, and only glass should be used; static electricity build-up on plastic can pull grains of the medium off the surface. If the work is not matted (some don't require matting for esthetic reasons), liners or narrow spacers should be used to separate art and glass.

Oil and acrylic paintings. These usually require frames that are more substantial than those used for other mediums. The frame should emphasize the positive character of oil or acrylic, yet be tasteful and simple in profile. The frames used vary as widely as painting styles, ranging from highly ornamental wood frames, with or without liners, to the wood strip frames favored by many contemporary artists and museums exhibiting modern art.

The frame must be strong enough to support the stretched canvas and prevent it from warping. Otherwise, movement will eventually crack the paint. A canvas on a stretcher frame has a depth of at least $\frac{3}{4}$", and you will find it's easiest and most pleasing to use a frame that is as deep as or deeper than the stretcher.

Photographs. A photograph is somewhat different from other art forms because the emulsion on the surface can be scratched and marred by fingerprints. In contact with glass, this same emulsion can support the growth of molds that will irreparably damage the print.

Photographs are difficult to keep flat, and unless the print is by an Ansel Adams or an Edward Weston, most framers dry-mount the photograph to some type of rigid mount.

Unless printed on resin-coated paper (has a plastic feel to both surfaces), photographs can often be flattened in a heat press. Once a print is flattened, glass and a mat will keep it as flat as any other type of paper art.

A wide range of choices is open to the framer of a photograph (see pages 22–27); the no-frame appearance of floaters, matted and unmatted, metal frames, and narrow through wide wood frames are among the possibilities.

Reproductions. Reproductions usually are framed just about as you would the original, with two exceptions. The first is that the frame should not be as heavy as for an original, since the color values may not have the strength or dimension of the original. The second is mechanical: most reproductions must be mounted to prevent warping. If yours is a reproduction of an oil or acrylic, and you're framing it without glass, protect the surface with varnish or sprayed lacquer.

Just because the cost of a reproduction is small, don't make the mistake of choosing framing that has a cheap look. A carefully framed reproduction can be a pleasure to behold, but one that is cheaply framed looks like just that—a cheaply framed reproduction.

Some framers maintain that reproductions present a new art form and should be framed in a modern manner. Most reproductions are used as items of decor, so use your own judgment in selecting framing that is pleasing to you.

Diplomas and other official documents. If you value the piece and want it to be around for a long time, use the same conservation techniques as you would for a piece of original art (see page 72).

You may want to forget the traditional narrow black frame and white mat. Try a natural wood or even a molding with a colored finish; colored matboard is another possibility. To make document framing still more interesting, professional framers often color the bevel of the mat or add a few thin lines around the bevel with a pen.

Rubbings. While some purists might challenge the thought that rubbings are art, they are becoming increasingly popular items in room decor. They also present some rather unusual challenges to a framer.

The selection of mat and frame is difficult as rubbings are often monotone—one color. A double mat can be effective, with the band of color in the inner mat just strong enough to accent the rubbing. Because ordinary mats appear flat alongside the textured surface of the rubbing, fabric-covered mats are often used.

More challenges: rubbings on thin paper wrinkle easily, the paper is seldom flat to begin with, and the process of rubbing induces stresses and even wrinkles and small tears. So a rubbing will seldom lie flat when framed. Mounting is not recommended as it will obscure the embossed quality of the rubbing and the natural characteristics of the paper.

Needle art and fabrics. Most pieces are stretched on a rigid backing before framing. But if the material is stiff enough, you can frame it with glass, backing, and mat, as you would a piece of paper art.

If matboard looks stark next to the material you're framing, you might cover the mat with a suitable fabric.

To glass or not to glass is an issue among people who frame needle art. Some maintain that glass obscures the richness and texture of the fabric. Others are more concerned with the protection afforded by the glass. If your material is old, fragile, or very valuable, frame it under glass.

Tapestries, weavings, and rugs. Usually these have enough weight to hang flat, and it is only necessary to support the piece along the top edge. If the piece is fragile or very valuable, enclose it in a glass-faced cabinet on the wall. The calendar case on page 30 can be scaled up to about 2 by 3 feet. Larger cabinets are best left to professionals. Another possibility is a frame similar to the one on page 32.

Among methods available to support hangings: a metal or wood rod stitched to the back and resting on hooks in the wall, or a pocket sewn on the back to hold the rod; nylon self-gripping fastener attached to the hanging and the wall; and the wood clamp shown on page 33.

Guidelines for framing

Restraint or initiative—which path to follow? You can actually take both routes, because in framing design they can eventually lead to the same goal: good taste. You are different from an extemporaneous public speaker whose words enter irretrievably on the record. You have more latitude than a set designer who confounds opening night critics. As the one who ponders what frame combinations to use, you can experiment and change your mind until you have what pleases you most, yet does not steal attention from the picture.

The guidelines we offer here are based on known design concepts, yet they are also points of departure when you feel moved to unfold your imagination. For definitions and illustrations of the various framing parts discussed here, see the special feature "What's What in Framing," page 55.

Proportion. When you think about a definition of proportion, "A part considered in relation to the whole," its implications are hard to nail down. But when you see examples based on the art of picture framing, proportion falls into place. Here are tips:

• The smaller the art, the wider the frame. This holds especially true with bold mediums—tiles, enamels, intensely color-saturated paintings. With objects such as these, frames whose moldings are as wide as the artwork would be proportionate.

• Large paintings, whether representational or abstract, look best in narrow moldings.

• Narrow moldings are used with wide mats or wide liners. Conversely, wide moldings should have narrow mats or liners. A typical combination would be a 4-inch molding and a ¾-inch insert. Reverse those

(Continued on page 60)

Framing without frames

Sleek and simple, with the look of today, the "frameless frame" is ideal in certain situations. Though not meant to supplant other kinds of framing, this method is quick, relatively inexpensive, unobtrusive, and highly changeable, making it perfect for use with posters, mounted photographs, children's art, and the temporary treasures of people whose tastes are evolving.

Frameless frame systems come in several treatments, in both metal and plastic. To use them, you sandwich your picture between glass (or acrylic) and a mounting board, then fasten everything together with brackets. Some systems will also accommodate one or more mats. Or you can mount the art on heavy mounting board and display it without glass. One caution on the use of glass: newly cut glass can have edges that are dangerously sharp. Grind those edges on your own oilstone or have a glass shop do it for you.

You'll find the brackets or clips and the ties necessary for frameless framing all packaged together and available in art supply and variety stores. You'll need to supply the glass or acrylic, the mounting board, the mat, and of course, the art. The following information will help you decide which of the variations to choose—variations having to do with brackets and clips.

Corner brackets. One type is not unlike the paper corners that hold snapshots onto album pages. These brackets fit over the corners of the layered assembly, with only a little of the bracket visible from the front. They're secured by ties either around or diagonally across the back—metal bands or spring-tightened cords. The crossover design is intended to ease stress on the picture. Whichever one you choose, you should avoid overtightening the ties lest distortion occur.

Another type of corner bracket system, designed to prevent distortion or warping, involves the use of edge and corner brackets. The system consists of eight transparent plastic parts, four of which are cleated, four that are flat. Each cleated piece fits into a flat member to form an L-shaped—or crossed—unit with clips at the ends of both pieces. Thus, eight unobtrusive ends peer over the edges of the picture, two to each side. The pairs are secured to the frame by a spring-loaded cord that forms a rectangle after it's looped around the clip assembly junctions.

Edge brackets. There are two of these clips per picture, but they're wider than corner clips and fit around the top and bottom edges. Secured by a tie threaded between them, they're less obtrusive than corner clips, but the design puts some strain on the assembly.

"Swiss" clip. This system consists of four or eight edge clips, not secured by a tie. Instead, each spring-loaded clip has a tooth that is gently tapped into the backing, which must be of a soft, easily pierced material. The retainers that peek over the edges of the picture are so narrow as to be almost unnoticeable. An additional piece in this kit is a bracket, also tapped in, to hang the picture or to accommodate a stand.

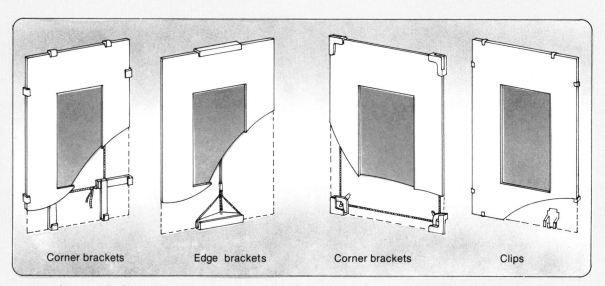

| Corner brackets | Edge brackets | Corner brackets | Clips |

Brackets and clips *allow you to display artwork quickly without frames.*

. . . Continued from page 58

measurements for an example of a wide mat/narrow molding combination.

• Some pictures have more "weight" than others. A painting of a crashing surf has more weight than one of a flower centerpiece. Therefore, select a powerful frame for the ocean scene, a simpler one for the still life.

Additional guidelines to proportion are offered in a later section headed "Mats."

Moldings. These can be integral parts of the art or they can stand away from it. Whatever, they should neither overwhelm nor underwhelm the picture. And they should bolster the color and composition of the artwork. Some examples:

• Many representational and surrealistic paintings have images that seem to recede from you. This special depth deserves a molding that slants deep into the work, emphasizing that quality. A *deep scoop* is an example.

• Abstracts are often flat and two-dimensional. For these, try moldings that slope toward the wall at their outer edges but thrust the picture into the room. *Reverse bevels*, which are severe and plain, will work well with angular subjects, while the softer *swan* or other rounded high-rabbeted moldings will show off abstracts that have free-floating forms.

• Seascapes mate well with coarsely grained wide moldings stained to resemble driftwood.

• Impressionistic paintings have a special luminosity that goes well with delicate white or gold moldings.

• Post-impressionist works, such as the paintings of Van Gogh, need strong moldings to express their power, but they should be simple, not ornate.

• Fundamentally simple paintings work best with plain moldings, but heavily detailed art calls for highly ornamented, richly designed frames. For some examples, see pages 20 and 21.

• Large, bold, rustic paintings expressed with heavy brush strokes require strong moldings with simple finishes. Another approach would be to use a frame of rough-hewn, weathered, sturdy wood that is butt-joined rather than mitered.

• Moldings with color give more enclosure to the art than do natural woods. But you can have both grain and color in your frame by choosing molding finished

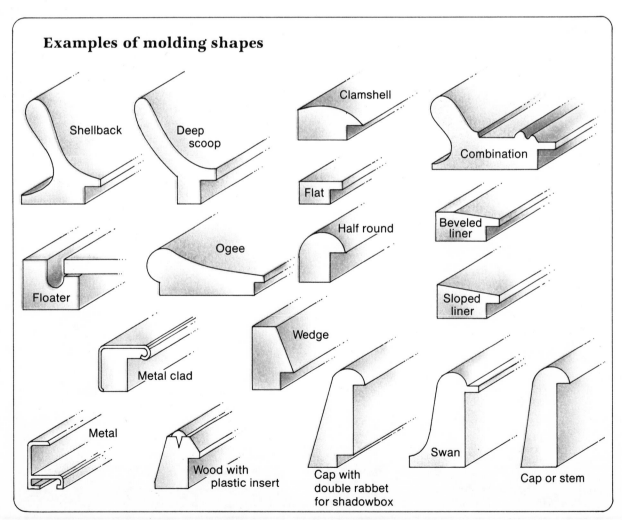

Examples of molding shapes

Shellback

Deep scoop

Clamshell

Combination

Flat

Floater

Ogee

Half round

Beveled liner

Sloped liner

Metal clad

Wedge

Metal

Wood with plastic insert

Cap with double rabbet for shadowbox

Swan

Cap or stem

Best selection *of finished moldings is found in frame shops. Building supply outlets may have both finished and unfinished moldings.*

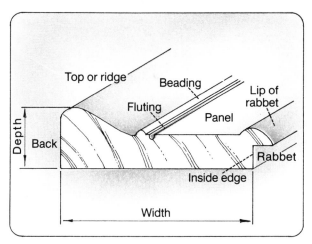

Molding nomenclature is special language. Knowing it helps you communicate with the framer.

with a colored stain. Paint and lacquer finishes, on the other hand, will give you color with a no-grain look.

Liners and fillets. These "frames within frames" are moldings keyed to serve as *inserts* into the outer moldings. They often look as if they were part of the outside frame, since they are used mostly with oil or acrylic paintings (or their reproductions) and needlework, which generally don't require glass. They lend separation by a strip of color or texture, and they soften the transition from picture to frame. Liners are sometimes gilded, often fabric covered, even painted.

Some framers reserve the *fillet* designation for a narrow second liner frequently installed next to the artwork. It is often gold leafed for warmth or silver leafed for a cool effect. Fillets also give a "finished" look by means of a highlighted bead on the edge closest to the art. In all, they give the frame extra sparkle.

Should you use a liner rather than a mat for paper art? Yes, if you want to try for a more formal, traditional, possibly antique effect than you can get from most mats. A liner that is separated from the outer molding by glass looks especially rich. For examples of liners and fillets, see pages 4–47.

Mats. These eye-pleasing windowed components are good examples of the maxim, "Form ever follows function." The practical purpose of a mat is to keep paper artwork from touching the glass, where damaging condensation, mold, and fungus can form. Yet, functional as they are, mats are important design elements. They provide space around the art that keeps it from being crowded by the frame. And they isolate the artwork so that the viewer's eyes can focus readily. Here are some tips on the use of mats, dealing first with color, then with proportion:

Remember how the frame can change a picture's color? Well, a picture can change a mat's color, too. A gray mat can actually lose its grayness just by picking up a color from the picture.

But also notice how a mat color can alter the mood

of a picture, can make it seem warm and lively or cool and calm. Experiment—try samples of mats with different color intensities. A strong one may just overwhelm a gentle picture, while one a touch lighter can provide precisely the right contrast to make the picture emerge confidently.

Given two mats of the same width, notice how the dark one will envelop a picture and a light one will let it expand (see page 56).

A mat emphasizes its own color in the picture. Make sure this is what you want—often it's just great, but sometimes it distorts the picture's composition.

Room light affects mat color. Incandescents give it one quality, fluorescents another.

The size of the mat affects the impact of its color. A wide mat of intense color could be too forceful, but a narrow mat of the same color could give the contrast you want.

So much for mat colors. Now how about the proportions?

First of all, there's no standard mat border size, though $1\frac{1}{2}$ to $3\frac{1}{2}$ inches is considered wide, and less than $1\frac{1}{2}$ inches is thought of as narrow. One wider than $3\frac{1}{2}$ inches is perceived as large, yet quite appropriate when the arrangement permits. Fact is, a 4 or 5-inch mat will lure a viewer toward a very small artwork, one that might be passed over if it had a small mat and frame.

When you use more than two mats, make sure that no two exposed widths are the same and that each width differs from the width of the frame and from any other frame feature, such as a panel. Otherwise you'll get a staircase effect.

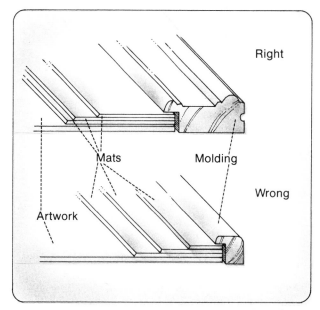

Vary the widths of framing elements to slow the eye as it moves from the surroundings to the art.

Customarily, especially on pictures hanging low on the wall, the bottom border of a mat is cut a bit wider (usually $\frac{1}{2}''$) than the sides and top. If you want to emphasize verticality—an Oriental scroll or a portrait of a standing figure, perhaps—make the long side borders narrower than those at top and bottom. Similarly, you can emphasize other shapes. Make an artwork look wider, for example, by cutting the mat with the sides wider than top or bottom.

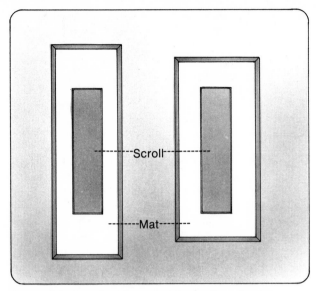

Emphasize the shape of the art by selecting mat proportions that accentuate it.

Where do you place a square picture in a vertical frame? Try one professional's system: Cut one-third of the mat window below the center line of the complete mat, two-thirds of it above. Here's how to do it: Let's say your picture is 4½ inches square and your mat is 9 by 12 inches. Divide the height of the picture into three equal sections, that is, 1½ inches each. Divide the height of the mat into two, placing the horizontal center line at the 6-inch mark. Lay the picture over the mat so that the lowest line (the one 1½ inches from the bottom, 3 inches from the top) coincides with the mat's center line.

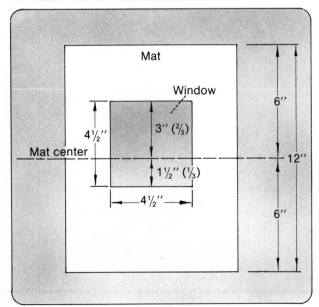

Here's one way to position square art.

Another design note about mats: Ever wonder if that tiny 6-inch etching or watercolor that you cherish could be displayed so it could be seen and appreciated? Try it in a dramatically outsized mat with border 4—even 5—inches wide. It will look great. One enthusiast actually framed his favorite postage stamp that way and finds his friends zeroing in on that "artwork" as eagerly as if it were an original Rembrandt.

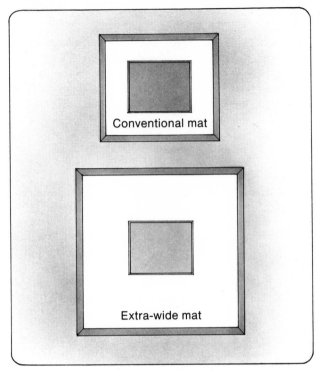

Draw attention to a small picture by framing it in a dramatically oversized mat.

Last of all, don't be afraid to experiment and break the guidelines. Visit some of the galleries and frame shops in your area, and you may discover many examples of innovative framing that defy traditional guidelines.

You may find art framed with a mat wider at the top instead of at the bottom, or with the picture placed off-center. Perhaps you will see a tiny, exquisitely rendered watercolor seeming to float on a mounting board, and the wide mat that surrounds it cut so that the art is located near the bottom of the window, with the mounting board as a backdrop.

In another gallery, you may find a similar work with a double mat, yet the inner mat is invisible and serves only to separate the outer mat from the mounted art. Worrying about the staircase effect? One framer didn't—he framed a work so that the width of the art, mat margins, and frame were all the same.

These designs had two things in common—they broke traditional guidelines and they all were attractive. Because of the framers' willingness to use imagination and taste, the framed art appealed. And that is good design.

Techniques for Framing

Once you've decided on the design of your framing—the number, color, and texture of the mats, and the style and finish of the frame molding—you're ready to go ahead with the framing of your art.

This section covers measuring and cutting techniques, mat making, mounting the art, making the frame, and assembling everything ready for hanging. Though it is directed primarily at people interested in doing their own framing at home, those who decide to patronize do-it-yourself framing shops or custom framers will find much useful information in the pages that follow.

The framer's tools & work space

Whether you choose to do the whole framing job or only part of it, you'll need work space and tools.

Your work table should be spacious—about 30 by 60 inches; it should also be firm and have a smooth and rigid top. Fastening the legs to the floor with angle brackets will make it even sturdier. The height should be such that you can work comfortably at it while standing. Thirty-six inches is standard, but you may wish to adjust that up or down to suit your own preference.

The table should be situated so that you can walk around it; ideally, it should be under a skylight or near a north window. If you need artificial light, use fluorescent lighting that approximates daylight; otherwise the colors you're working with will not appear true.

When cutting mats, you'll want a slightly cushioned surface to work on. Mat or mounting board, a sheet of synthetic shoe sole material, and a special cutting pad available from art supply stores are all satisfactory.

The basic tools are those that are essential to cutting a mat, mounting a picture, building a frame, and assembling all the components. With these and some practice on scrap materials, you can produce work you'll be proud to hang in your home.

Additional framing tools—listed on page 65 as "helpful"—will enable you to do better quality work with less effort if picture framing becomes one of your hobbies. And why shouldn't it? Framing is the fillip that can turn a painting into poetry, an inexpensive poster into a work of art—accomplishments that bring pleasure even to professional framers with many years of experience.

Tool quality

The prices and quality of tools vary widely, even among products with the same brand name. One well-known tool manufacturer offers tack hammers ranging from $3 to $15. The same company lists miter box and saw combinations as low as $30 and as high as $250. So which tool to buy?

Of course your budget for framing tools must be considered. But whatever your budget, stay away from cheap tools made by unknown manufacturers. The bargain tool seldom lasts long, it dulls quickly, and it may lack accuracy. Generally you will be better off to buy the lowest priced name brand item than an unknown at any price.

Name brand tool manufacturers offer tools at several quality levels, and usually price is an indication of quality and accuracy. For most home framers, buying tools in the middle of the price range is the best choice. Of course, if the top of the line is on sale at an irresistible price, don't resist.

Basic tools for framing

Included here are the tools you must have to do all the steps in framing a picture. Some may be in your tool box already. And if you have a table or radial-arm saw you won't need a miter box and saw. But more about power saws later.

Brushes. You'll want some brushes for wet mountings. Some will be used to spread adhesives (a 2 to 3-inch paintbrush will do), another wide one (could be a wallpaper brush or a 4-inch or wider paintbrush) will be used to brush the print flat. You'll use still another to tap away at wrinkles and air pockets so that the entire surface of the print will adhere to the mount. Start with a 1-inch paintbrush, from which you will cut off the tip bristles to make it firm enough for this purpose.

Drill and bits. You'll need either a hand drill or push drill to make pilot holes for the nails that secure the corners while the glue dries. You will also need drill bits, sized so that the holes will be about 75 percent of the nail's diameter. Some framers use the next smaller nail chucked in a hand drill to make the holes. This technique is all right with soft wood moldings but is not recommended for moldings made of such hardwoods as oak and chestnut.

Glass cutter. You may buy your glass cut to size or design your framing to fit a standard size. But a glass cutter is invaluable if you already have some glass you want to use. Treat a glass cutter as you would any other sharp tool, and protect the cutter from damage.

Hammer and nailset. An upholsterer's hammer, a heavyweight tack hammer, or a lightweight claw hammer will be needed to drive the brads into the corners of the frame and into the back of the molding to hold the backing in place. A nailset is used to drive the nail heads below the molding surface at the corners (the holes are later filled with putty or wax to blend with the molding). Some alternates to these tools will be found on page 65.

Miter box and saw. Sometimes you buy these as separate items, sometimes as a set. As one isn't much good without the other, they are handled as a set here.

The wood and metal set used to build the frame on page 85 was from the middle of the price range; it cuts accurately when used with care, and it will give several years of use; more expensive sets include all-metal miter boxes with stops and clamps. The metal construction gives greater accuracy, and will do so for years. The stops and clamps contribute to accuracy and make the miter box easier to use. The saws in these sets are made of high-grade steels that maintain their sharpness even after extensive use.

You can cut frame moldings in the lowest priced hardwood miter box, but the wood slots that guide the saw wear quickly, resulting in miters that do not fit tightly.

The miter saw is a specialized form of the back saw. Both have metal reinforcing along the back of the blade to keep it from bending. But many back saws are only 12 inches long, too short for use in a miter box. Buy a back or miter saw at least 16 inches long, and choose one with 12 or more teeth per inch.

Before you use your miter set, bolt or clamp the box to your work table.

Miter clamp. This is the tool that holds the mitered ends together while you glue and nail the molding. It is adequate for moldings up to 3 inches wide. (Larger moldings require one of the clamping devices described under "Helpful tools for framing," next page.) You can build a frame with only one of these clamps, but their cost is low and you may find it more convenient to purchase four so that you can leave the corners clamped until the glue dries.

One version of this inexpensive clamp (see below)

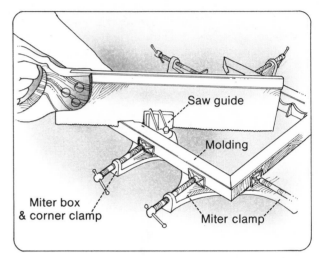

Miter clamp with saw guide can substitute for a more expensive miter box.

Basic tools for framing pictures

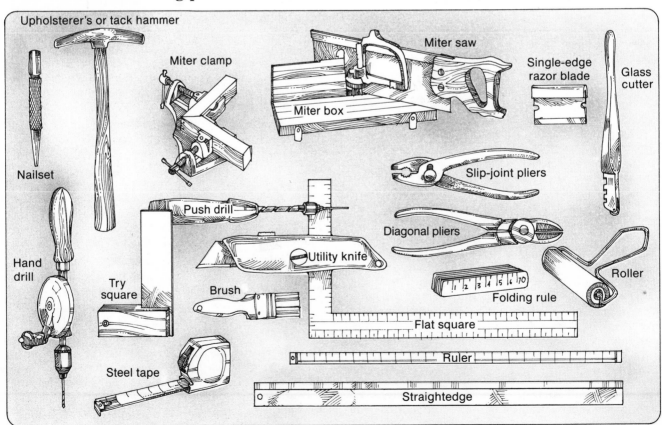

is equipped with saw guides so that you can use it instead of a miter box. Though not as accurate as a miter box, the device works fairly well with small moldings.

The homemade *string clamp* is an inexpensive clamping device made of ¾-inch or thicker L-shaped plywood or hardwood blocks. Cut a ¼-inch-wide groove around the outside edges and drive a wood screw partly into the wood. These keep the string in position on the blocks. Turn to the project on page 96 to see how to use these clamps.

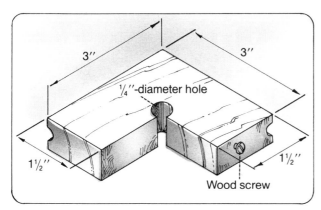

Four blocks, *shaped like this, and string make inexpensive set of miter clamps.*

Pliers. Two kinds of pliers are handy for framing—a small pair of diagonal pliers for cutting wire and a pair of slip-joint pliers. The latter can be used for pulling out the nails holding the backing if you reframe a piece of art, pushing in those same nails (see page 90), or removing a nail that bent while being tapped into place.

Roller. You will want a 4 to 6-inch rubber roller, also known as a brayer, to roll the art out flat when you're mounting with adhesive. For applying glue, some framers prefer a particular type of paint roller over brushes. This is the small roller designed to paint close to the corners of walls and ceilings, and to paint trim.

Rulers. You must be able to make accurate measurements to ⅟₁₆ of an inch. Whether you use a steel tape (6 feet is long enough), a carpenter's folding or zigzag rule with an extension at one end, or a metal yardstick depends on personal preference or which one you already own. All are adequate, provided they are graduated in ⅟₁₆-inch increments.

For cutting mats and other cardboard components, the metal yardstick can be substituted for the straightedge shown on the facing page. However, because it's narrow, it's harder to hold, and because it lacks a 45° edge, it doesn't work well for making bevel cuts with a knife.

Squares. The large square, known as a carpenter's or framing square, is used in the making of mats, mounts, and backings. It should be graduated in ⅟₁₆-inch increments on both the inside and outside edges of the two legs. Short pieces of masking tape affixed to the underside of the square will prevent it from slipping or marring the mat.

The smaller square shown on page 64 is a try-square. If you already have a combination square, use it—it's just as good for checking the corners of the frame for squareness after you assemble it.

Straightedge. If you intend to cut more than a couple of mats, invest in a good straightedge to guide your knife or mat cutter. Straightedges in lengths up to 45 inches are available from art supply stores or by mail from framing suppliers. They are about 2½ inches wide and ⅜ inch thick and are usually made of stainless or plated steel. One edge is at 90° to guide a knife or mat cutter, and the other is at 45° to guide a knife in a bevel cut (the angle of the blade in mat cutters can be adjusted).

Be sure to buy a straightedge that is long enough for your needs; the added cost is much less than buying a second straightedge when you have a large mat to cut.

As with the large square, a few pieces of masking tape stuck on the bottom of the straightedge will prevent it from slipping while you cut.

Utility knife and razor blade. The utility knife is used in several frame-making tasks. One is trimming excess wood and splinters from miter cuts. Another is cutting acrylic sheet sometimes used instead of glass (a special blade is available for this task). The last is cutting the paper products used in framing: matboard for mounts, cardboard for backing, paper for dust seals and paper mats—and, with practice, cutting mats.

For safety, buy one with a retractable blade and be sure to retract the blade when you're not using the knife. Paper dulls a sharp edge quickly, and if you want neat mats you must keep the blade sharp. You can sharpen the blade on a small oilstone, but most people find it more convenient to throw a dull blade away; replacements are inexpensive.

A razor blade comes in handy for finishing incomplete mat cuts (see page 74) and trimming mat imperfections.

Helpful tools for framing

Most of these tools are specialized framing tools of low to moderate cost; a few are tools more generally used. The specialized tools are representative of those available, but the list is certainly not all-inclusive. There are many more, including the expensive choppers, frame saws, mat cutters, and mounting presses used by professional framers. Cost of this professional equipment is in the hundreds—even thousands—of dollars.

Should framing become a serious avocation, you may want to investigate these specialized framing tools, for they can help you do a better job with less effort. Tailor your purchases to your frame-making needs, though. There's no point in buying an expensive mat cutter if you intend to make only a few mats.

Some nonessential but helpful framing tools

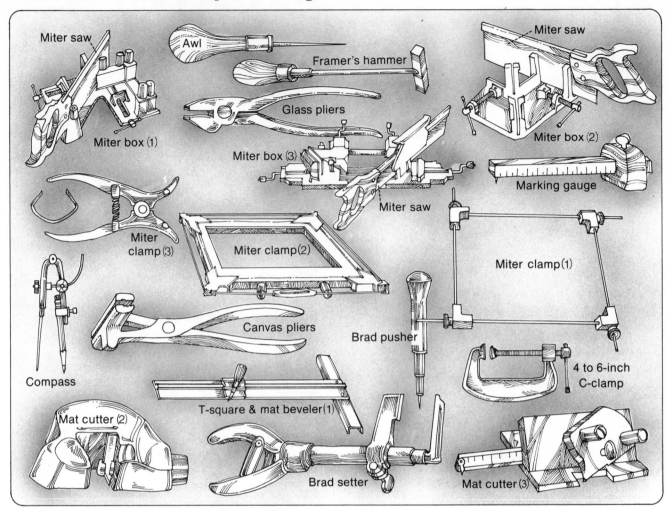

Awl. This carpenter's tool quickly makes pilot holes for screw eyes or other mounting hardware.

Brad pusher. This handy tool can replace the hammer and nailset for nailing frames and backings. The tip is recessed to hold the brad. Pushing down on the spring-loaded handle drives the nail into the wood. Pressing the handle down as far as possible countersinks the head of the nail.

Brad setter. This professional framer's tool is used to push brads into the molding to hold the backing in place.

Canvas pliers. The serrated jaws of this tool (also known as webbing or leather pliers) grip the canvas or other heavy fabric while you pull it around the stretcher bars and fasten it.

C-clamps. Though not essential, several 4 to 6-inch C-clamps are useful. You can clamp the miter box to the work table or clamp a molding in place while you cut it.

Compass. The compass is used in the same way as the marking gauge to mark mat windows.

Framer's hammer. Sometimes known as a sprig, this little hammer does the same job as the brad

setter. The angle of the handle and the rectangular shape of the head make it easier to use for this purpose than a tack hammer.

Glass pliers. The jaws of these pliers are designed to hold the glass with a minimum of pressure so that you can break off a narrow strip of glass after scoring.

Marking gauge. The use of this tool to mark the cutting lines for a mat window is shown on page 70. The gauge comes with a steel point that must be replaced with a pencil lead.

Mat cutters. Three typical hand mat cutters are shown. One unit (1) comes with a T-square for laying out the mat and guiding the cutter. Another, mat cutter (3), has a built-in marking gauge to mark mat windows, but cuts only 45° bevels. Like mat cutter (2), whose blade can be adjusted to make cuts from 45° to 90°, this cutter must be used with a straight-edge.

Miter boxes. Woodworking supply catalogs list several miter boxes that bear little resemblance to the classic one shown under "Basic tools for framing." Boxes (1) and (2) are typical and are basically the same, with guides for 45° and 90° cuts and with clamps to hold the work.

Miter box (3), specifically designed for frame-making, has guides for cutting 45° miters, as well as two pairs of clamps so that you can join two of the frame corners at once. Clamps and guides can be positioned on the graduated base so that the moldings are cut to length without additional measurements.

Miter clamps. Of the three illustrated, two are based on the same principle as the homemade string clamps shown on page 65. With clamp (1), tension is applied to the corners with threaded rods and thumb nuts. Several sizes are available; the largest can clamp frames measuring 48 by 48 inches or 36 by 72 inches. Tension is applied to the corners of clamp (2) by a cable tightened with a turnbuckle.

Clamp (3) is derived from the clamps that framers made from spiral upholstery springs. Known as wire clamps, they are sold in sets of four, in six sizes that have holding capacities from $\frac{3}{8}$ inch to $3\frac{1}{4}$ inches. Depending on the size of the molding, one, two or even three may be used on each corner. As shown below, the special plier known as a spreader spreads the sharp points so that the clamp can be applied to the corner. These same points usually leave larger indentations than countersunk nails, marks that are more difficult to fill and hide.

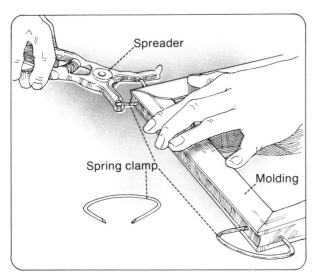

Apply spring clamp by spreading with special tool and releasing when clamp is in position.

Power saws. Fitted with fine-toothed, hollow-ground planer blades, table and radial-arm saws are handy if you are "mass-producing" frames, but don't go out to buy one just yet. A portable power saw, on the other hand, is too unwieldy for frame-making.

Extra care is required when cutting miters with a power saw. The whirring blade tends to move the molding along a table saw's miter gauge or a radial-arm saw's guide fence, ruining the miter. Clamping the molding or using a stop block can prevent this movement.

Many saw manufacturers' instruction books and other books about power tools give instructions for making a miter gauge for your saw that holds the molding securely and allows you to cut an accurate 45° miter every time.

You can make the gauge shown below to use with a table saw. The two guides must form an exact 90° angle and be at an exact 45° angle to the line of the saw blade. First the moldings are cut square to the same lengths as the outside dimensions of the frame. Then each end of each piece of molding is cut at a 45° angle in the gauge, one end at a time.

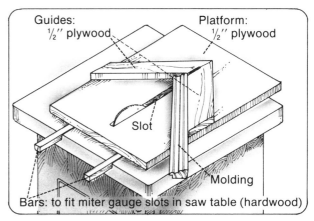

Miter jig is designed for table saw use. For radial-arm saw, use basic design without hardwood bars.

Woodworker's vise. If woodworking is your hobby, you probably have a woodworker's vise mounted to your workbench. Just pad the jaws with carpeting and you have a miter clamp that can handle moldings of many shapes.

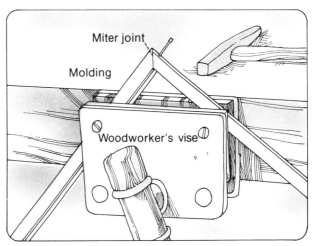

Use woodworker's vise to clamp mitered moldings when joining them.

Wall arrangements display treasures, enliven rooms

You may be pondering how best to display several art pieces that share a common theme, as well as similar frames or identical size. Or you may be casting about for a scheme to show works that vary widely in subject, trim, or dimensions. Either way, a planned wall arrangement provides an attention-grabbing, compliment-gathering answer. Don't be too concerned with the supposed lack of commonality in the second example—the very act of grouping creates a relationship among the pieces you display.

Here are guidelines to attractive picture walls, as well as a note or two on pitfalls to avoid.

Locations

Room walls are the most obvious places for picture arrangements. But groupings have a way of enlivening areas we often take for granted—surfaces often resigned to dullness. Fact is, you can make veritable galleries out of usually ignored spaces in your home.

Hallways. With selective lighting, these can sometimes be better places for wall arrangements than certain rooms. For one thing, halls are usually furnished simply, if at all, and consequently they are free from clutter. For another, they are often long and narrow, so that arrangements hung at the ends have the benefit of being viewed from some distance. Walls that run the length of a narrow hallway are ideal for pictures that can be enjoyed from a closer vantage point.

Stairways. Besides the decorating aspect, pictures can have the wholesome effect of relieving the tedium of climbing those stairs yet another time. And who knows? They may even slow the mad descent of youngsters by making them pause to admire, or at least ponder, the newest addition to the wall. Enclosed stairs don't allow room to appreciate large paintings, but open ascents may well offer space for one piece in the grouping that is so commanding as to get attention from admirers in the room below.

Guidelines for wall arrangements

Tasteful groupings can be symmetrical or seemingly random, but they are always planned. One way to plan is to make cutouts the actual sizes of the pictures and then use masking tape to arrange and rearrange them on the wall until you get a scheme that pleases you. Then the taped-on cutouts can be used as templates when you install picture hooks. Or work with the cutouts on a large sheet of paper placed on the floor, and transfer the whole thing to the wall as one large template. Dark pictures should be represented by dark cutouts.

Another way is to draw a scale model of the complete wall—furniture and all. Then cut out scale models of the pictures, sketching outlines of the mats, as well. A one-inch-to-one-foot reduction is manageable and easy to compute.

Here are some guidelines to help you as you experiment with arrangements.

Alignment

Though your pictures may be of different sizes, arrange them so that the linear components—the frame outlines, mat edges, occasionally even elements in the compositions themselves—relate horizontally or vertically, or both.

Balance

Here, especially, is where your cutouts will help. Arrange and rearrange them until you are sure that large balances small, dark balances light. Let your own taste and feelings guide you. This is called *informal balance.*

Formal balance results from massing works of equal "visual weight" on both sides of an imaginary vertical line. Visual weight refers to color, size, or intensity of subject as well as other more subtle factors that you can often judge by eyeballing.

Align *various linear components—mat and frame edges.*

Visualize a tree

This guideline suggests you group your pictures in the shape of an imaginary tree, using a large vertical artwork as the trunk and letting other pictures branch out from it. Take care, though, to think of your tree as a windswept cypress or a meandering oak rather than a perfectly crowned elm or a tall redwood—that kind of symmetry seldom makes for free, comfortable groupings.

What to avoid

There are few "wrongs" in art grouping, since it is a subjective and personal accomplishment. But there are two things specifically to avoid—too-tight grouping, and overcrowding.

If you have but a few pictures to assemble, try to space them so as to fill a predetermined space, with plenty of "air" circulating around them. Use a piece of furniture—a sofa, perhaps—to set outer limits, and try to have the outermost pictures come reasonably near those limits. On the other hand, if the result would be a "strung-out" look, you may want to choose a smaller piece of furniture to set the limits.

Overcrowding can result from trying to group too many pictures into a space. Stay within your predetermined limits, but also establish a maximum height under which you can hang your pictures. Art hung too high will be difficult to see. Adhere to another rule that says your prime subjects should hang at eye level—and in a room where people are generally seated, not standing, that means not too far above eye level for the person who is sitting down. And of course, no picture should be placed so high that viewers have to crane their necks to see it.

Informal balance of large and small, hung in relation to imaginary centerline, makes pleasing arrangement.

Formal balance around imaginary centerlines is often best arrangement for frames of same size.

Visualizing a tree on your wall can help you arrange frames of varying sizes.

Overcrowding of many pictures on a wall detracts from appearance of individual pieces of art.

Making mats

Professional framers rank making mats as one of the most stimulating aspects of their work. The mat has more impact on artwork than any of the other frame components, and because it is so important, it requires even more care and esthetic consideration than any other framing element.

Tools you'll need

Of the basic tools (see page 63), you'll need a ruler, folding rule or steel tape, large square, straightedge, utility knife and extra blades, a razor blade, and a sharp pencil.

Materials

What are mats made of? Cardboard and ragboard, principally. Cardboard is a wood product and is the material most commonly used for mats. But wood contains acids that will in time leave permanent discolorations where they touch the artwork. Wood-free matboard, like the very finest stationery, is made of 100 percent cotton fibers—hence the name, "ragboard." Framing in which only this acid-free material contacts the artwork is known as "conservation framing" or "museum framing" (see page 72).

But ragboard is costly and comes in a limited range of colors, mainly neutrals. Standard (cardboard) matboard, unlike the solid makeup of ragboard, has a cardboard section laminated to a sheet of colored paper on the top and a neutral-colored sheet on the bottom. Usually the bottom sheet is purely structural, helping to strengthen the pulpy cardboard, but sometimes it too is colored.

Cardboard mats are available in a variety of textures and coverings. Some are embossed with the look of fabrics—silk, linen, burlap; others have a pebbled or wood-grained appearance. Mats covered with fabric, foil, or cork are also made, but these are difficult to cut, and covering your standard mats with fabric or other materials, after cutting, may turn out to be preferable.

Though you'll be working mostly with paper-based matboards, you may one day want to experiment with other materials. Dare to be different. Glass mats (see page 41) are not uncommon, and even metal mats have been used. One novel "mat" is really no mat at all: the artwork is sandwiched between two sheets of glass or clear plastic, leaving a mat-width transparent border through which the background wall can be seen (see page 12). This system is fine if the artwork is not valuable or if moisture is certain not to be a problem.

Measuring & marking

Accuracy is crucial when you measure and mark dimensions on matboard. The slightest inaccuracy will make the mat appear crude no matter how skill-

fully you cut it, so check and recheck your work as you go along.

The very first step is to check the corners and edges of the matboard, since these will guide your measuring and your cutting tool. If the outside corners of the mat are not exactly 90°, the window you lay out with a marking gauge or by measuring from the edges of the mat will also be out of square. And once the framed picture is on the wall, you'll be aware of the distortion every time you look at the results of your work.

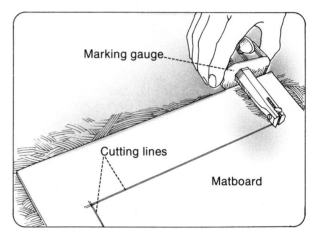

With a marking gauge, *you're assured window corners will be square if the mat corners are 90°.*

Don't assume that your picture is square. Measure across the two diagonals—the corners are square if the measurements are the same. If not, and if you plan not to cover the edges of the picture with the mat, you may have to compensate when laying out the mat window. You can do this by cutting the window out-of-square or cutting it larger to show margins of ½ inch or more. If you want the mat to hide the white margin around the picture, be sure to measure the width and height of the picture at several places and use the smallest dimensions when figuring the size of the mat window. The edges of the window should cover the edges of the art by ⅛ inch to lessen the chance of any white border showing and to make alignment easier.

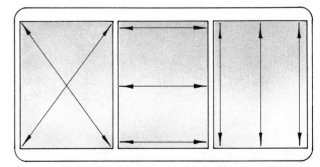

Take several measurements *of picture in all directions to determine correct mat size.*

Some professionals feel that window cuts made from the front of mats have sharper edges than cuts made from the back. But erased pencil marks have a way of showing up in oblique light, as do burnished areas left by some mat cutters. Because of that, we believe that cutting from the back is both safer and easier, and that is the procedure followed in this book.

Another precaution in marking the mat for cutting: Because matboard tends to respond to moisture in the air and therefore expands, you must allow space (about ⅛ inch) between the inner edge of the frame and the edge of the mat. Leave a similar space between the edges of the frame and those of the mounting, backing, and glass.

If, as is done in this book, you cut the mat first, make the frame larger than the mat. If, on the other hand, you already have the frame, cut the mat and other components smaller than the frame.

Mat cutting

The sheer linear perfection and clean corners of a well-cut beveled window are adequate rewards for the work and care you put into it.

Whichever type of cutter you use, practice on scrap materials until you are satisfied with your work. Be sure to cut some corners—this is the way to become proficient in stopping the blade at just the right spot. Here are some points to remember:

• The blade in a mat cutter is adjusted for bevel cuts, so be sure to use the 90° edge of the straightedge to guide the cutter. If you use a knife, you will choose between the 90° edge and the 45° edge, depending on the cut you want.

• Keep the blade sharp either by changing frequently or sharpening on a fine-grit oilstone. Paper products dull a sharp cutting edge quickly, and the result can be ragged cuts.

• Keep the cutting edge moving at a steady pace, stopping quickly at corners. Slowing down as it nears the corner may change the character of the cut. You want to avoid overcutting if at all possible, but the blemish from overcutting is small, visible only on close inspection after the framing is completed. If you do stop short of the corner, complete the cut with a razor blade.

• Move the cutter with your whole body, not by flexing your arm. This makes it easier to cut a straight line at a steady pace.

• The tip of the blade should project through the matboard just enough to penetrate the mat and mark the material underneath.

In the event that you've chosen to use a utility knife guided by your straightedge, you can quickly acquire the necessary skill by practicing on scrap matboard or any inexpensive thin cardboard. Here's how to do it:

Just to get the feel of the equipment, start by making some straight cuts, using the 90° edge of the straightedge as a guide. Lay the side of the blade against this edge, with the cutting edge at 45° to the matboard. Pull the knife along the straightedge with just enough pressure to cut through the matboard and make a mark on the underlying material.

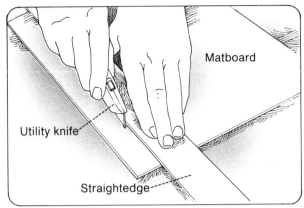

*Making a **straight cut** with a utility knife.*

Now mark some corners with pencil and square. Practice cutting these, cutting both to and from the corners.

Turn the straightedge around and use the 45° edge as your guide. With the blade slightly inclined toward the bevel, make several practice cuts. Continue tilting the blade more and more until it lies against the 45° edge.

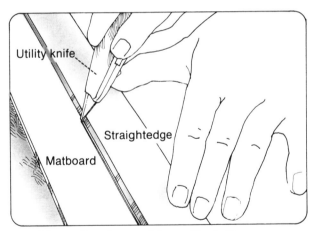

*Making a **bevel cut** with a utility knife.*

Having mastered a straight bevel cut, graduate to beveled corners. Once comfortable with these, you're ready to cut your first beveled mat.

Why the beveled edge? Three reasons. First, it leads the eye to the picture. Second, it gives a pleasing illusion of depth. Last, straight cuts cast shadow lines on the artwork if the light source is oblique.

But the vertical cut has its place—in the double mat arrangement. Even a reverse bevel is used to give the effect of a straight cut, but without the shadow.

(Continued on page 73)

Conservation framing

In Venice and Florence, pollution erodes precious statues. In California, a university library mishap soaks priceless first editions. Regrettable realities. Yet, unwittingly, we allow similar desecration in our own homes because we don't use conservation framing (also called archival or museum framing) for valued works. Even custom framers occasionally forget to warn of the damage ordinary framing can inflict on valuable art, so do ask about it.

Canvases have their own special needs—they require cushions to prevent rubbing damage by the frame, and double-thick backing to protect the canvas from punctures (see below).

But the concern here is principally with the most potent, yet avoidable enemy of paper art—the *acidity* that is present in all wood and wood-pulp mats, mounting boards, and backings.

What paper art is valuable?

You should consider the finest protection for just about everything that is not a print or a reproduction. Works of value include original watercolors, drawings, etchings, fine art photographs, certainly diplomas and awards. The list goes on and on.

Nonacidic framing

When a wood frame is the appropriate choice, don't substitute other materials to avoid wood's acidity; artistic integrity would suffer. Instead, make sure the frame doesn't contact the artwork. But to isolate with wood-derived mats is self-defeating; within months, their edges leave calling cards in the form of linear stains. Fortunately, there are alternatives (shown below).

• Acid-free mats. Use neutral pH board or museum board. Once available only in shades of white, it now has a widened color range. If you use a regular mat over the acid-free mat for color as shown below, seal the cut edges with shellac or other sealer.

• Conservation mounting. Hinge the mat to a ragboard mounting board, using linen tape. Hang the artwork from the mounting board with hinges of rice paper (torn, not cut, to avoid sharp lines) glued with wheat or rice starch paste. All of these materials are acid-free. Hinging art to mat is equally acceptable, as is use of hinge materials and pastes that are acid-free.

• Backing. Even though the mounting board isolates the art, don't use a corrugated board backing. This highly acidic material wreaks damage, given the slightest chance, even permeating the acid-free mounting board. Use strong, double-thick mounting board for a backing that provides physical as well as some chemical safety.

Proper sealing. Airborne sulfur dioxide converts to sulfuric acid when absorbed into paper. To get as near an airtight frame as feasible, make sure the dust seal remains intact and that the glass-to-frame contact is secure.

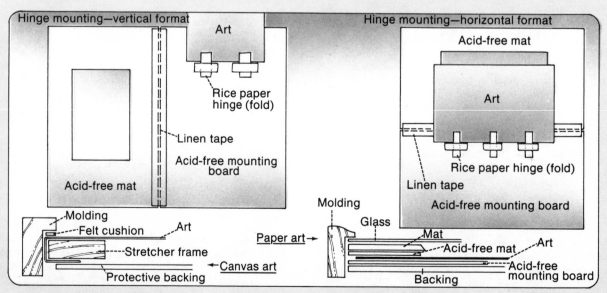

Conservation framing can help protect your valuable art.

Some mats you can make

Now that you've mastered the art of measuring, marking, and cutting mats, it's time to make some.

You can adapt the mat projects that follow—single and double mats, covered mats, and multiple-window mats—to most framing situations you may encounter.

Once you're comfortable making these, let your ingenuity and imagination run free, creating your own mat configurations and decorations. Should your flights of fancy take you to round, oval, and other nonrectangular windows, be a little bit wary. By all means try cutting them if you wish, but remember that professional framers have both the equipment and experience and can give you a finished mat with none of the frustrations you will encounter if you cut your own.

Single mat. First measure the actual size of the picture you're about to frame. For purposes of this example, let's assume it is $11\frac{1}{4}$ inches wide by $14\frac{3}{4}$ inches high. To hide any white margin around the image, make the mat window slightly smaller so that $\frac{1}{8}$ inch is covered on each side. Thus the window size will be 11 by $14\frac{1}{2}$ inches. Suppose that after considering proportions (see page 58), you decide on a

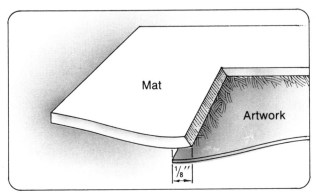

Overlap hides white edge around picture and holds art against mounting board.

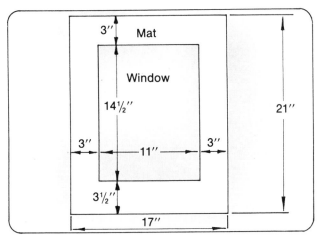

Measure and mark cutting lines on back of matboard.

mat width of 3 inches on the sides and top and $3\frac{1}{2}$ inches on the bottom. Add these to the window dimensions to arrive at a mat size of 17 by 21 inches. For the sake of simplicity, these same sizes will be used in other examples of mats and frames that follow.

Though the matboard you purchased should be exactly 90°, we recommend that you check the corners with a large square to be sure. Remember, if the outside of the mat isn't square, the window won't be either. Then, using a pencil and the ruler (you could also use the square or T-square), mark the cutting lines for the outside of the mat.

Now make a vertical cut along the lines, using the straightedge and a utility knife or mat cutter. Check the corners with your square before going on to the next step.

Lay the mat face down, then measure and mark the lines for the window, using the square to guide your pencil (you can also use a ruler, T-square, or marking gauge).

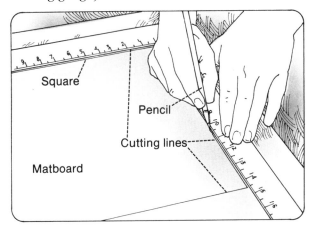

Large square can be used to measure and mark cutting lines for mat and window.

With the straightedge as a guide, use the utility knife or mat cutter to make a bevel cut along the pencil lines, being careful not to overcut the corners. If you use a utility knife, the straightedge should be on the lines. With a mat cutter, position the straightedge so that the blade cuts along the line.

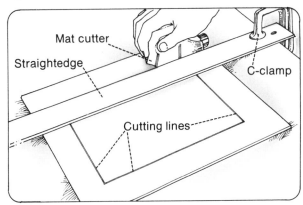

C-clamp prevents straightedge from slipping when you are using mat cutter to cut window.

If you cut short of any of the corners, use a single-edge razor blade to complete the cut and then lift out the center of the mat (save it to use for a smaller mat or for practice).

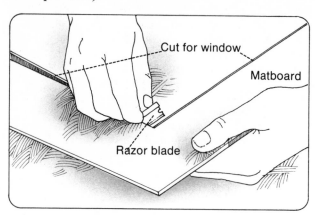

Use a razor blade to finish the cut if cutter stopped short of corner.

Check the edges of the cut. If there are any rough spots, smooth them with a piece of number 220 sandpaper or the fine surface of an emery board. Now your mat is ready to use.

Double mats. A single window opening with two mat edges showing (there can even be three or more, as shown on page 16) is a design feature that allows you to expand your creative spirit. You can bevel one or more—many framers bevel all the edges, because the effect of two, even three, beveled edges showing is exciting and eye-catching.

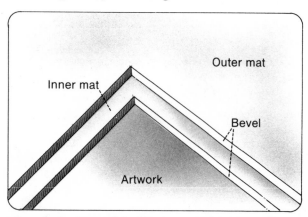

Beveled edges of double mat are pleasing to the eye.

The mat closest to the picture is usually a darker color than the outer mat, lending additional trim to the artwork. The visible portion of that inner mat should be quite narrow, just enough to provide an accent. You accomplish this by cutting the window of the inner mat $\frac{1}{2}$ inch to 1 inch smaller than the outer window, leaving a dark border of $\frac{1}{4}$ to $\frac{1}{2}$ inch. The outer mat will display lots of border, but only an accent strip will show from the inner mat.

Duplicate the dimensions given for the single mat, making a window size of 11 inches by 14$\frac{1}{2}$ inches for the inner mat. Assuming that you wish a $\frac{1}{2}$ inch border, add twice the border width ($\frac{1}{2}$ inch) to the window size. The result is 12 by 15$\frac{1}{2}$ inches—the window size of the outer mat, which will have margins of 2$\frac{1}{2}$ inches on the sides and top, and 3 inches on the bottom.

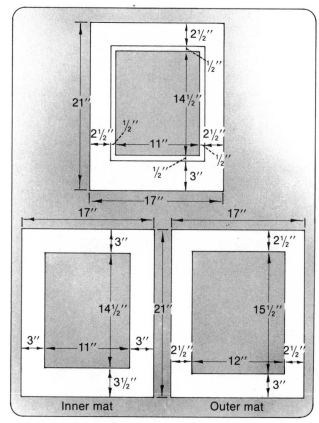

Make a dimensioned drawing of the double mat, then make separate drawings of inner and outer mats.

To make the double mat, first cut the matboard for the outer mat to 17 by 21 inches. Then mark and cut out the 12 by 15$\frac{1}{2}$-inch window for that mat. Save the piece you cut out—you'll need it. Apply double-coated tape close to the window edge of the back of the mat, but don't let the tape overlap the edge.

Now cut the matboard for the inner mat $\frac{1}{4}$ inch smaller—16$\frac{3}{4}$ by 20$\frac{3}{4}$ inches. This will assure that the measurements for the window will be made from the edges of the front mat. If the two mats were the same size, they might not line up exactly when you stick them together. The result would be disaster—the width of the border would be uneven. Center the inner mat over the outer mat and lay it gently face down on the taped back of the outer mat. Be sure to check the centering before you apply pressure; now turn the two-mat assembly over.

Here is where you use that piece you cut out. It will serve as a temporary base for the next cutting job: making the smaller window in the darker mat. Lay a

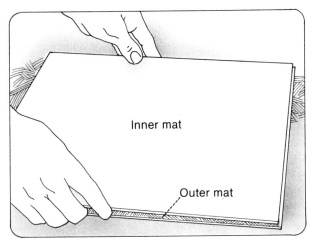

Center smaller mat *face down over taped back of outer mat; press down.*

piece of double-coated tape in the middle of the back of the cutout and fit it into the window from which it was removed.

Once again, turn the taped-together mats over. The back of the inner, as-yet-uncut mat will be facing you. Mark the smaller window (11 by 14½ inches) and cut it out. Both cutouts will come out together, since they are held together with tape.

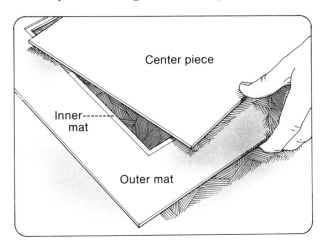

Mark and cut *inner mat window; remove cutouts.*

The result? A handsome double mat, especially good-looking because the bevel of the outer mat, bound to be lighter in color than the mat itself, affords an extra contrast strip against the dark lip of the inner mat.

For even more drama, you can make a three-mat arrangement, but remember to cut the three windows so that the mat borders are unequal—no two should be alike. Otherwise, you'll create that staircase effect shown on page 61.

A tip from the pros. Should you wish to make a double mat with a narrow, unbeveled inner mat, you can use paper in place of matboard for the inner mat. Any heavy paper will do, but most pros cut narrow strips of matboard and peel off the colored paper.

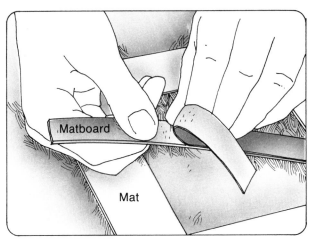

With knife blade, *lift corner of colored face paper from matboard strip and peel off.*

After you cut the outer mat, lay it face down on the work table. On the back of the mat, mark the edges of the inner mat on two opposite sides. With double-coated tape, fasten a strip of colored paper to the back of the mat, being careful to line up the edge of the paper with the marks. On larger mats, also check the alignment from the front to be sure that the width of the exposed colored paper is uniform. Repeat for the opposite side. Next mark the remaining opposite sides and apply the paper strips. Now turn the mat over and admire the effect.

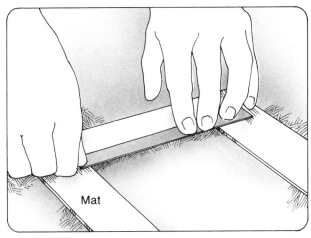

Line up *edge of paper strip with marks on back of mat, then press down on double-coated tape.*

Multiple-window mats. The time may come when you'll want to display family photographs or a set of equal-sized small color prints of a special-interest subject all in one frame (see pages 15, 17 and 19). Your first challenge will be to select a mat in a shade that will enhance the colors in all of the pictures. Then group them on an uncut matboard to get a feel for the proportion of the windows relative to the borders. A good rule is to arrange the prints so that the mat borders *around* the total grouping will be larger than the borders *between* the prints.

Once the arrangement pleases you, mark the window openings on the back of the mat and cut them out. An example is shown below. Whether you cut each window separately, or first make all the vertical cuts and then all the horizontal ones, is a matter of personal preference.

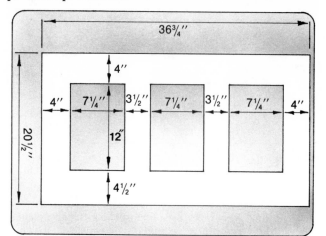

On back of mat, *measure and mark windows.*

Assembling a row of larger, vertical-format pictures in a long horizontal frame (see page 17) is another rewarding project. Try to select prints that can be accommodated in equal-sized windows without losing too much subject matter. This grouping may well call for matboard bigger than is available at your art store or frame shop; 32 by 40 is as large a standard mat as you likely can find, yet your project may require a mat 60 inches or longer. The six-window mat shown on page 17 is 70 inches, too long to cut from a single piece of matboard. It could have been cut from two pieces butted together and then covered with fabric. Instead, a stronger mat was made by cutting it from a single piece of ⅛-inch hardboard, which is available in sheets up to 48 by 96 inches.

Fabric-covered mats. The character and texture of fabrics lend a special cachet to many artworks. Your taste will guide you about which colors will best enhance your picture, but a safe rule is to stay in the neutral range.

Which fabrics to use? Whatever is consistent with the mood of the picture. Burlap would be eminently appropriate for a rustic scene—a rusted farm machine, or a weathered barn. Grass cloth sounds ideal for a Japanese still life or a Tahitian beach. Linen and silk are more formal—perfect for an Oriental scroll, a rubbing, an elegant botanical print. (Silk, incidentally, should be dry-mounted, a process best left to professionals; see page 79.) And don't overlook the amazing varieties of fabric-textured wallpapers.

Professionals differ about what materials to use in mats that will be covered. The best choice for the long haul seems to be matboard of a color close to, but not darker than, the fabric.

Illustrated below is a simple, effective system for covering mats:

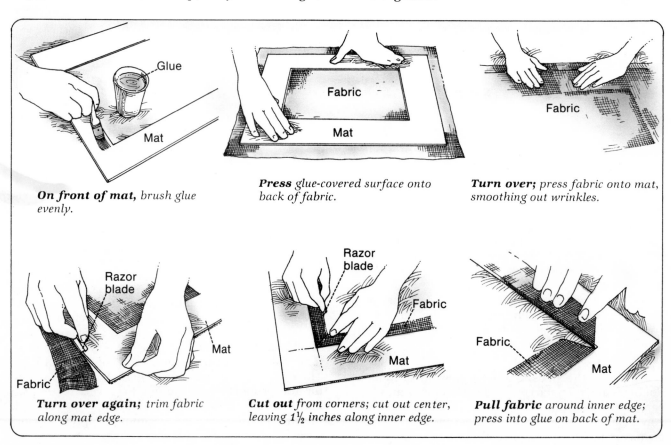

On front of mat, *brush glue evenly.*

Press *glue-covered surface onto back of fabric.*

Turn over; *press fabric onto mat, smoothing out wrinkles.*

Turn over again; *trim fabric along mat edge.*

Cut out *from corners; cut out center, leaving 1½ inches along inner edge.*

Pull fabric *around inner edge; press into glue on back of mat.*

Mounting the art

Some form of mounting is needed to keep the art properly positioned in the framing. This section gives you the pros and cons of different mounting methods and shows you how they are accomplished. Be sure to read the special feature "Conservation framing" on page 72.

Mounting: the pros & cons

Fabric-based artworks—such as oil paintings, batiks, and needlepoints—have to be mounted, and so do some pieces of paper art, but the methods used are quite different. Paper art can be attached to a rigid backing with adhesive, but fabric art is usually stretched over a frame, a method known logically as "stretching." You may also have occasion to mount three-dimensional objects, and you'll need a certain amount of ingenuity to do this in an unobtrusive manner.

With paper art, mounting is permanent and it drastically reduces the value of original art, since the art cannot be removed from the backing and returned to its original condition. For fragile or damaged pieces, you'd be wise to turn the job over to a professional framer.

There is no choice but to mount some other types of paper art. A notable example is a photograph, because it's almost impossible to make a photographic print lie flat. Creased and wrinkled paper artworks, even originals, also are candidates for mounting, as the creases and wrinkles can be minimized, if not eliminated.

Some artwork is best displayed "floated" on the mat, so that the edges of the art are visible, with the mat color and texture showing behind the art instead of in front of it. This type of mounting also provides a quick and inexpensive method of displaying a picture without a frame.

Tools you'll need

Of the basic tools (see page 63), you'll need a large square, ruler or folding rule, straightedge, utility knife and extra blades, and a sharp pencil. You'll also need a sheet of plate glass large enough to more than cover your longest mounting job, with enough overhang on the front of your work table so you can lift one end. Usually available from a glass installer who rescued it from a broken store-front window, it has flatness and weight that makes it an ideal place under which to slip a newly mounted work. Place the glass on a base of felt or similar soft material.

You'll want some brushes for wet mountings. Some will be used to spread adhesives (a 2 to 3-inch paintbrush will do), another wide one (could be a wallpaper brush or a 4-inch or wider paintbrush) will be used to brush the print flat. You'll use still another to tap away at wrinkles and air pockets so that the entire surface of the print will adhere to the mount. Start with a 1-inch paintbrush, from which you will cut off the tip bristles to make it firm enough for this purpose. A painter's trim roller can be used to spread adhesive, too.

A roller—or its rollerlike cousin, the woodblock printer's brayer—and a soft squeegee will come in handy. Some substantial felt-bottomed paperweights are good to have around.

Mounting materials for paper art

Some mounting methods, notably dry and vacuum mounting, require expensive equipment; others, such as wrap-around wet mounting, demand considerable skill. These are best left to the professional framer. Even so, there are enough other methods to meet most of the needs of the home framer, and the materials they require are fairly modest.

Mounting boards vary widely. Matboard works for many applications. For more rigidity, there's Upson board, a thicker material. Hardboard, even plywood, are used, though they may prove too heavy in some instances. There's a foam plastic, covered on both sides with kraft paper, that is rigid, light, and easy to cut. There are ragboards, commonly known as museum boards, to use in conservation mounting. The list has not been exhausted; your art supply dealer or custom framer will have more to show you.

Adhesives for home workroom use include vegetable glue, grain pastes (wheat and rice), and spray-can adhesive. Stay miles away from rubber cement; when its solvent ultimately dries, it loses its sticking power. White household glue is acceptable except for conservation framing.

Several spray adhesives are available, including those meant for photographs, cloth, cardboard, felt, and practically any other material. They are not recommended for mounting valuable works and, because they lose their adhesion with time, are not considered permanent by professional framers. The most common use of this method—mounting photographs—is illustrated on the next page. Be sure to check with your photographic dealer for the correct type of spray to use with your picture, and follow the manufacturer's directions on the can.

Tapes? They're useful for temporary holding, and for mounting for temporary exhibits. Tapes with adhesive on both sides and tapes that transfer a ribbon of adhesive are particularly valuable in assembling double mats and sticking the dust cover to the back of the frame. Unless specifically labeled as chemically neutral or acid-free, tapes should not be used in contact with original art.

Still another adhesive is available for mounting photographs and nonoriginal art. Adhesive sheets, plastic film coated on both sides with adhesive protected by peel-away paper, are available from art supply stores (see illustration on next page). One brand allows you to reposition the art, but most seem to reach out and grab your work—once the adhesive touches the surface, it is there to stay.

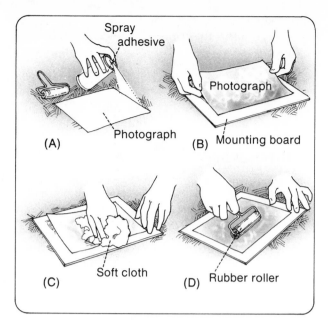

Spray adhesive mounting. (a) Spray adhesive on
back of photograph. (b) Position on mounting board.
(c) Rub with soft cloth. (d) Bond with roller.

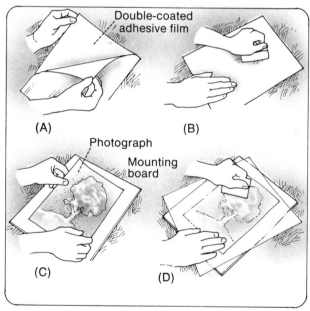

Adhesive film mounting. (a) Peel off protective
sheet. (b) Apply adhesive to photograph back, smooth
with cloth. (c) Remove other sheet, position photograph
on mounting board. (d) Cover photograph with paper, rub
to bond.

Mounting methods for paper art

Adhesive mounting, hinge mounting, and wet
mounting are the most-used mounting methods for
those who do their framing at home. Two other
methods, dry mounting and vacuum mounting, are
included here in spite of the fact that most home
framers would not care to invest in the equipment.
Still, they are among the easiest and most reliable
methods, and if you wish to dry or vacuum mount,
you can take your work to a do-it-yourself or custom
frame shop. Or a serious amateur photographer
friend may have a dry-mounting press.

Adhesive mounting. This is the most practical
method for the home framer who lacks access to a
dry-mounting or vacuum press. You apply liquid
adhesives to the print, not to the mounting board,
following the directions on the container. When the
adhesive is tacky, lay the print on the board and
smooth it out with brush or roller.

One difficulty with adhesive mounting is warping
—the paper shrinks as the liquid adhesive dries,
and the shrinkage causes the mounting board to
bend. There is a simple solution, though: *countermounting.* Dampen one side of a piece of kraft paper
with a moist sponge, spread adhesive on the other
side, and press it to the back of the mounting board.
As the kraft paper dries, it will exert a tension to
counter the pull of the drying print.

Do the countermounting process immediately after the print is mounted.

Smooth or roll the print on its board, working from
the center to the edges to ease out wrinkles and bubbles. Then slip it under your plate glass weight and
allow it to dry for the length of time recommended
by the adhesive manufacturer.

Hinge mounting. The preferred method for paper
art, hinge mounting is always used in conservation
framing unless the condition of the art precludes it.
As illustrated on page 72, the art is fastened to the
mounting board or mat with strips of paper called
hinges. The first strips are reinforced with more
strips laid across them. For adhesive, use one of the
liquid glues (see page 77). Some framers recommend
tearing the strips rather than cutting them, as the
frayed edges make a better bond. Though linen
tapes may be used as hinges, the paper ones are
preferred, because if the framed art is dropped,
the paper hinge will rupture without damage.

Wet mounting. This process adds a step—a tender,
painstaking, possibly even risky step—to the adhesive mounting system. But when a print has been
wrinkled, too tightly curled in a mailing tube,
creased, even torn here and there, wet mounting
can be worth the effort. If the art is original, you
might be better off to use the services of a professional framer.

A special use of wet mounting—a variation—is to
wrap the art around the sides of the mount. This is an
excellent way to show off a fine photograph, particularly with a mount that is at least a half-inch thick.

One caution: Not all inks are water-resistant. Test
a nonexposed spot on the print before you attempt
wet mounting. And of course wet mounting can't be
used for watercolors.

Immerse the print in clear water and gently
smooth it out, face down, on your clean sheet of plate
glass. Work with a brush, squeegee, or roller, or any
combination to smooth the paper, but be gentle, for
the wet paper is fragile.

Mounting

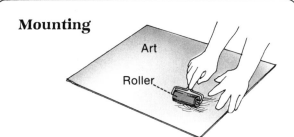

Apply adhesive *to back of picture.*

Fold *(pasted sides together), but do not crease.*

Turn over *and position one end on mounting board; spread flat.*

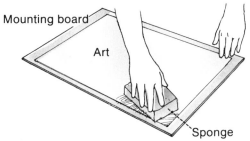

Sponge off *excess adhesive; with clean roller, roll smooth, working from center.*

When you have the imperfections smoothed out, spread liquid glue thinly but completely over the back of the print and also over the mounting board. Fit the board ever-so-carefully on the print, then fit a damp countermount (see directions under "Adhesive mounting," preceding) on the board. Turn the assembly over carefully and smooth out any imper-

fection you may have missed on the face of the print. Allow the assembly to air-dry until just moist, then place it under your glass weight. Don't forget to wash off the top of the glass while any stray adhesive is still wet.

Dry mounting. This is the system that rates highest in popularity, at least commercially. It is superseded in this book by the two preceding methods, only because it requires, for best results, a dry-mount press not likely to be found in the workrooms of home framers.

The adhesive used in dry mounting is a coating on both sides of a sheet of fine tissue placed between the art and the mounting board. Under the heat and pressure applied by the press, an excellent and permanent bond occurs. A recently introduced dry-mounting tissue is intended for use with color photographic prints, particularly those made on resin-coated papers. This type bonds at a lower temperature and the art can be removed later if desired.

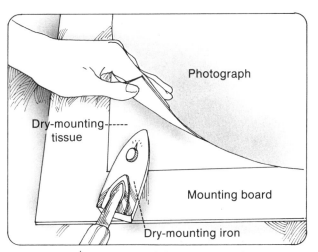

Position *photograph and dry-mounting tissue on mounting board. Lift photo corners; seal tissue to mounting board at corners with iron.*

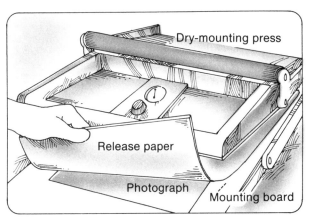

Place *in press; cover photograph with release paper. Close and bond for required time.*

Vacuum mounting. Vacuum mounting is another process that requires an expensive piece of equipment—a vacuum mounting press—usually found only in professional workrooms.

The work is attached to the mount board using the adhesive method. Then the mounted print is placed in the press between a rigid unheated platen and a soft, flexible diaphragm.

When the press is closed, the air is evacuated from the interior, and the weight of the atmosphere presses the diaphragm against the work. Any air trapped between the print and the mount is removed.

Vacuum mounting results in an excellent bond without wrinkles, bubbles, and other distortions in the art. It is particularly valuable with art that has been folded, creased, or wrinkled. Because not all framing shops have vacuum presses, you may have to shop around for one that can handle your work.

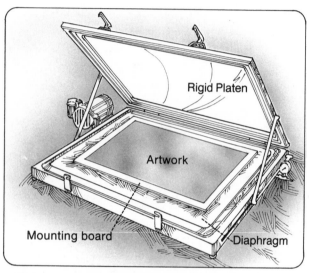

Vacuum-mounting press used by professionals bonds picture to mounting board under pressure and without heat.

Mounting fabric artworks

Be it an oil painting on canvas, an Indonesian batik, or an elegant textile, one accepted way of displaying it is to mount it on a flat frame of wood.

Artists usually make their frames from stretcher bars or strips available from art supply stores. Stretcher bars are stocked in standard lengths, and two pairs of appropriate length are required per frame. The design is such that wedges can be used to expand the frame slightly after the fabric is stretched, a feature that comes in handy to make the fabric drum-tight or to retighten it if the fabric stretches and sags over a period of time. The outer edge of a stretcher bar should be slightly thicker than the rest of the bar. This minimizes the possibility of damage to the fabric by the inner edge. Large stretcher frames should have securely fastened cross braces that do not contact the fabric.

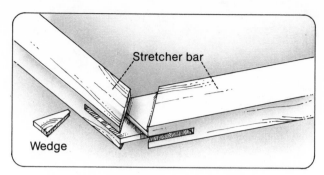

Artist's stretcher frame is ideal for mounting textiles, batiks, other fabrics.

How to mount fabrics. The basic method of mounting a fabric is to lay it upside down on a flat, smooth surface and place the stretcher frame on top of it. Starting at the centers of opposite sides, you pull the fabric around the frame sides and fasten it. As you do this, it's very important that you periodically check the front side to be sure that you are not distorting the pattern. The best way to avoid distortion is to pull with uniform tension.

Heavier materials such as canvas are more easily stretched with canvas pliers (see page 66). Grip the fabric between the jaws of the pliers, pull decisively around the stretcher, and fasten.

Tacks can be used for fastening the fabric, but a heavy-duty stapler available at hardware and building supply stores is an ideal tool for the purpose. The stapling method is illustrated below.

There are other methods for fastening stretched fabrics. One is to fasten opposite edges of the work with heavy thread laced back and forth across the

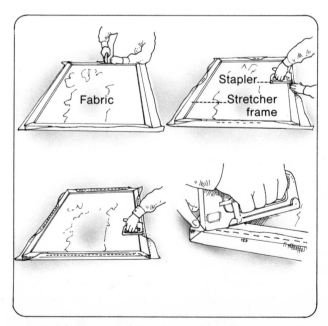

Pull fabric around frame and staple at centers of opposite sides. Staple from center toward corners, maintaining even pressure so as not to distort pattern. Fold material at corners and staple.

back of the stretcher or other mount. The method is known as *latching*. You latch in one direction, as shown, adjusting the tension to avoid distortion of the work. Then you repeat the process between the other two edges.

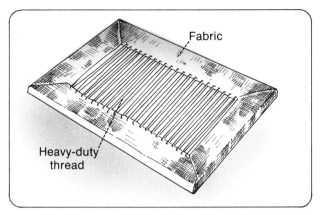

Mount fabric *by sewing back and forth between opposite edges pulled around back of frame.*

With another method, you fold the edges of the fabric over the back of a mounting board, fastening the fabric to the back of the board with strips of masking tape. Because the adhesive on masking tape loses its hold eventually, the fabric art should be framed between a liner or mat and the backing.

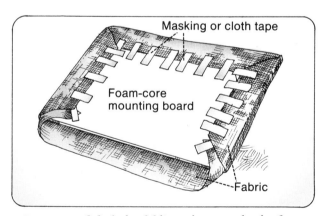

Or mount fabric *by folding edges over back of mounting board and taping them in place.*

Two fabric situations require somewhat different handling—old oil paintings on canvas, and needlework that lacks extra material around the borders.

Old oil paintings. These usually challenge framers in either of two ways: the painting is too old and fragile to withstand the agonies of stretching, or there is not enough extra canvas to grasp and pull around the stretcher bars.

The solution is the same—glue the painting to a new piece of canvas. You might check with the curator of your local art museum for an experienced conservation framer and restorer.

Needle art. Needlepoint and other fabric art with too little extra material to pull around the stretcher bars can be mounted in your choice of two ways.

You can sew a width of extra material around the border and then stretch and fasten it in the usual way (see page 80). Or you can stretch the needle art on a piece of Upson board, which is quite rigid but only ¼ inch thick. Staple near the edge of the work, being sure to hold the gun so that the staples go straight in.

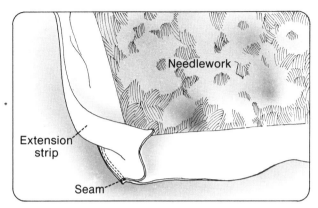

Extension strips *can be sewed to fabric art that's not large enough to go around stretcher.*

Mounting 3-D objects

Mounting a three-dimensional object requires both imagination and ingenuity, particularly if it is a valuable piece. Certainly you don't wish to do anything that might damage it or otherwise decrease its value.

Each object will have its own mounting method, which you'll determine after examining and carefully considering its shape and material. The attachment methods that follow will cover most situations, and examples in the photo gallery (pages 4–47) will help you solve your particular mounting problem.

Wire and thread. These materials offer an unobtrusive and safe way of mounting many objects. A loop of thread or wire encircles the object; each end is passed through a small hole in the mount, then tied or twisted.

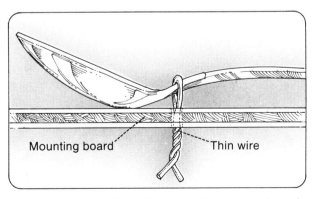

Mount spoon *by threading ends of wire loop through two small holes in mounting board and twisting tight.*

Mounting hardware. Should you have coins, dishes, spoons, small weapons, or similar objects that you wish to mount, you can buy fixtures made for that purpose. If you can't find what you want locally, a mail order source of frame supplies would be your best bet.

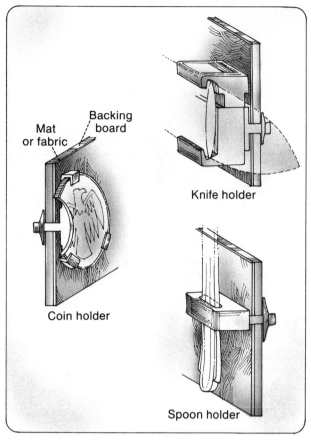

Mat or fabric

Backing board

Knife holder

Coin holder

Spoon holder

Specialized hardware is available to mount coins, cutlery, plates, similar objects; three examples are shown here. Some standard hardware can also be used.

Adhesives. Several types of adhesive are available that lend themselves to mounting solid objects.

• *Silicone rubber adhesives*, popular among professional framers and available in tubes from hardware, automotive, and building supply stores, are strong adhesives that work with a variety of materials. Unless your art is porous, the silicone rubber can usually be removed cleanly if you want a change later.

• *Double-coated tapes* with plastic and foam cores work well if the surfaces to be joined are smooth and flat. But if you try to mount a plate on a burlap-covered mount board with double-coated foam tape, the plate will be on the floor before you ever get it hung on the wall.

• *Various glues* can be used to mount your 3-D art if they're compatible with the materials to be joined (read the manufacturer's directions) and if you're not concerned with possible damage to the art.

Building the frame

Among those who work with wood for a livelihood—carpenters, cabinetmakers, boatbuilders, and others—no one person commands more admiration than the one who can fasten two pieces of wood in a snug, virtually invisible joint. Though there are some dozen recognized types of wood joints, the one most frequently used in frame-making is the *miter* joint.

What you will need to build frames with professional results are the right tools, a knowledge of basic math, a mental picture of how the finished product will look, a fair amount of time and patience, and a little practice on scrap lengths of moldings and liners.

In this section, you'll learn to estimate the amount of molding needed, measure and mark it for cutting, cut the miter joints, and glue and nail the molding into a frame that fits the mat you cut on page 73.

Where to buy your molding. As mentioned on page 50, obtaining the molding you want can be a challenge. Some professionals will not sell molding stock to home framers, and the choice at lumberyards is limited. If you shop around, you eventually will find a professional framer who will deal with you and may even cut the miters.

If you buy molding by mail, be sure to order enough extra to cover any defects in the molding (see page 94). Usually an extra 25 percent is enough.

If you can't find picture moldings in your area, you might try mail-order sources. Woodworkers and some molding supply companies advertise in hobby and craft magazines, so send for their catalogs. Some companies will sell you a set of samples at a reasonable price. Be sure to order enough extra to cover any defects in the molding. Usually an extra 25 percent is enough.

Tools and materials you'll need. Of the basic tools shown on page 64, you'll need a miter box and saw, hammer, nailset, hand or push drill and bits, try square, steel tape, folding rule or ruler, and miter clamps (one will do but four are recommended).

You'll also need some brads for fastening the molding—a stock of 1, 1¼, and 1½-inch brads will do for most molding sizes. If you need something longer for wide moldings, use finishing nails. White glue, #180 sandpaper, and putty and other finishing materials as required will cover the rest of your material needs.

Measurement & layout

As with laying out and cutting mats, accurate measurement is essential if your frame is to appear well made. Remember: Measure it twice, saw it once.

From the information that follows you'll learn how to calculate the size of the frame to fit your matted picture, estimate the amount of molding to buy, and lay out the cutting marks on the molding.

Estimating the molding needed. First determine the actual size of the frame needed, as measured between *rabbets*. Add $\frac{1}{8}$ inch to each dimension of the 17 by 21-inch mat to arrive at the frame size of $17\frac{1}{8}$ by $21\frac{1}{8}$ inches. (This allows for the clearance mentioned on page 71.) Carefully note those dimensions, as the project is based on them.

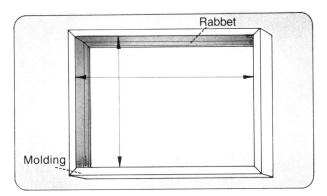

Measure frame size between edges of rabbets.

Let's assume that you have selected a molding for your picture that is $1\frac{1}{2}$ inches wide. You need to allow enough molding for the miters and for the kerf—the cut made by the saw blade. Allow the width of the molding for each miter cut—in this case, $1\frac{1}{2}$ inches, or a total of 3 inches per piece. Adding up, the length of each molding for top and bottom is $20\frac{1}{8}$ inches, plus $24\frac{1}{8}$ inches for each of the sides, for a total of $88\frac{1}{2}$ inches. Add 1 inch for the kerfs.

Molding is sold by the foot, so basically you need to buy 8 feet. But . . . even the best moldings may have imperfections, and many professional framers maintain that as inflation raises prices, molding quality goes down. So examine the stick from which your molding is to be cut. You will have to buy extra for any twists, warps, or other imperfections in the piece.

Should you be making another frame that consists of a molding, a liner, and a fillet—three wooden components in all—allow that $\frac{1}{8}$-inch glass clearance in the fillet only. Allowing two extra spaces would produce a loose assembly. If the liner is covered with a fabric that wraps around its height, however, allow for it in the molding rabbet and in the fillet's outside dimensions. If the fabric is velvet, $\frac{1}{8}$ inch is good. Thinner fabrics require less allowance.

Laying out the cutting lines. You have your molding and are ready for the next step in making your frame—marking the molding for cutting.

Moldings are seldom absolutely uniform in shape, size, and color throughout their length. The variations are minimal but can be an eyesore at the corners of the finished frame.

The cutting plan illustrated lays out the pieces sequentially as they are to be arranged in the frame. Only one joint (#1 in the drawing) can be mismatched, and if it's put at the top, it won't be obvious.

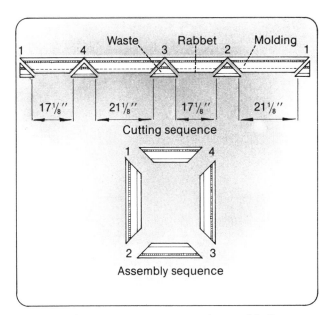

Make miter cuts in sequence and assemble frame in same sequence to minimize effect of variations in shape and color of molding.

As figured at left, the size of the assembled frame is to be $17\frac{1}{8}$ by $21\frac{1}{8}$ inches as measured between the rabbets. You start by cutting a miter at the right-hand end of your molding stock. All miter cuts are made with the rabbeted edge of the molding toward you. Detailed instructions for cutting miters below.

Now lay your ruler along the rabbet, the end carefully lined up with the cut end. Make a pencil mark on the rabbet at $21\frac{1}{8}$-inches and make an opposite miter cut at this mark.

Continue in this manner until all four pieces are cut. Be sure to mark the number of the cut on the back of the molding next to the ends as you proceed.

Cutting the miters

Before you start cutting, there are a couple of things you should do. The first is to fasten the miter box to the work table with wood screws or C-clamps. The second is to mark guidelines on the bottom of the miter box. This is done with a light kerf mark made by your miter saw in each of the two 45° positions. And be sure to make some practice cuts on wood scraps if you've never used a miter box.

Now you are ready to start. Adjust the miter box guide to cut a miter at the right-hand end of the molding. Place the back of the molding against the fence, with the right end slightly overlapping the kerf you made, as shown on next page. The molding will be easier to cut if you clamp it to the fence; use a C-clamp and a block of wood to protect the molding. Of course, if the shape of the molding precludes clamping, you'll have to hold it against the fence with your hand. You also should support the molding that projects beyond the miter box; some blocks of wood will do.

(Continued on next page)

. . . Continued from page 83

Place the saw in the guide and gently draw it toward you across the molding to start the cut. Stroke the saw back and forth across the molding with very light pressure, letting the weight of the saw do the work. Be careful not to apply too much pressure or the saw teeth will dig in and stop. Too much pressure also tends to tilt the saw, resulting in a miter that won't fit.

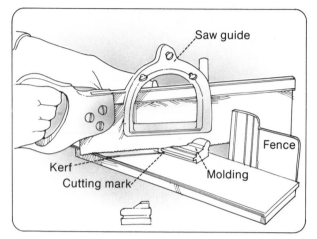

Cut miter *by stroking saw back and forth with only light pressure on it.*

With the end cut off, remove the molding and adjust the guide for the opposite miter. Mark #1 on the back of cut end. As shown below, mark your next cutting line on the face of the rabbet exactly 21⅛ inches from the freshly cut end. Remember to keep your pencil sharp—the finer the mark, the more accurate the work.

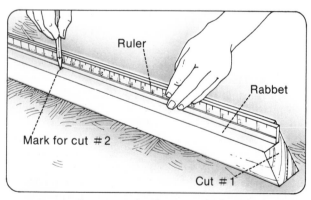

Measure for second miter cut *with end of ruler exactly on mitered end of rabbet edge.*

Put the molding back in the miter box, rabbet toward you and the back against the fence, and line up the mark with the edge of the kerf farthest from the center of the miter box. Always follow this procedure so that the kerf you make in the molding will be from waste material. Make the cut and be sure to mark #2 on the back of that end.

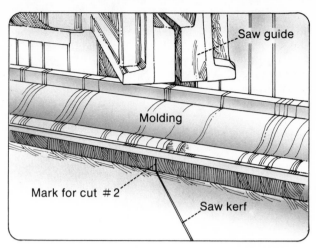

Line up cutting mark *with edge of kerf farthest from center of miter box.*

Now reset the guide and cut off the end of the remaining molding. Mark a new cutting line on the rabbet face exactly 17⅛ inches from the cut end. Adjust the guide for the opposite cut, line up the mark with the outside of the kerf, and make your cut. Don't forget to number the ends.

Continue until you have cut all four pieces; the next will be 21⅛ inches and the last 17⅛ inches.

Make one last check of your work. Place opposite pieces back-to-back to assure yourself they are the same length. Should they differ slightly, shorten the longer piece with sandpaper on a wood block wider than the molding, but be sure to preserve the integrity of the 45° angle. If the difference is substantial, you may have to make another miter cut, but first make sure you won't be altering your intended dimensions too severely.

Assembling the frame

The gluing and clamping instructions that follow describe the use of the inexpensive miter clamps shown on page 64. You could also use any of the other clamping devices described in "Helpful tools for framing" beginning on page 65; or you could use masking tape, as described on the next page.

Gluing and clamping. Lay out the frame members in correct sequence as shown in the drawing on the preceding page. This is to make certain you won't inadvertently join two sides of the same length. Even if the frame is to be square, this is worthwhile, since it assures that three of the corners will maintain continuity not only of color and shape but also of grain.

You can now reach for that dispenser of white household glue. Glue application is an area subject to dual theories. Some professionals advise you to apply the glue to both surfaces; others feel you achieve a better bond squeezing the glue onto just one. Both schools offer compelling evidence to support their theories.

Because the liquid absorption of different woods varies, we suggest you follow both schools. Apply a coat of glue to some of the scrap pieces of molding. If it is quickly absorbed, you will want to apply glue to both surfaces. If you're making a frame of pine builder's moldings, coat the surfaces, allow to dry partially, and then apply a second coat when you assemble the frame. Dense woods absorb glue but only slightly, and if your molding falls into this category, then coating one surface will suffice.

Make a dry-run by assembling the frame in the miter clamps without glue. Adjust each corner until you have the best fit possible; remember that the molding shape and color at corner #1 may not match exactly. Any last-minute adjustments to the miters must be made now.

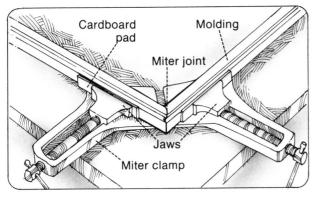

Pad jaws of miter clamp to protect molding while assembling frame.

Next remove the clamps from corners #1 and #3 and set aside. Loosen one stick of molding from the clamp on corner #2, apply glue, and reassemble for best fit. Repeat with corner #4.

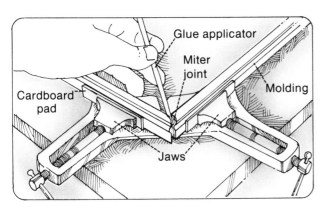

Apply glue to miter after loosening one jaw and sliding one molding away from the other.

Assemble the clamps on corners #1 and #3 without glue and with the best possible fit of the corners.

Now loosen one tightening screw on each clamp so that you can remove corner #4. Apply glue to the miter faces and reassemble.

If you have only one clamp with which to assemble your frame, join the corners one at a time. Place the moldings for one corner in the clamp and adjust for best fit. Loosen one molding, apply glue, and reassemble. After nailing (see next page), remove the clamp and join the opposite corner in the same fashion. One tip: Always put the longer molding in the clamp to your right; if you don't assemble both pairs in the same way, the frame will not go together. After completing the first pair of opposite corners, join the other two, being careful not to strain those that are finished.

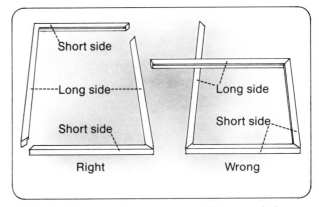

Assemble opposite corners with long and short moldings in same relative positions.

Some cautions on gluing: Wipe off excess glue with cleansing tissues immediately after joining each corner. On fabric-covered liners, apply glue only to the bottom of the miter so that when it oozes out—it always does—it won't stain the material. And use sparingly. As soon as you remove the clamps, clean off any excess glue and foreign matter from the rabbet. This assures that the glass will seat properly when you assemble it.

Masking tape. If a neighbor borrowed your miter clamps and didn't return them, or if you want to assemble several frames at the same time, try masking tape. Make sure you buy one that has some stretch to it—not all brands do. It is that stretch that provides the tension to hold the frame pieces in position. The method works particularly well with shapes such as floaters and other straight-backed moldings; you'll see cross sections of some on page 60.

Assemble the corner with glue, carefully aligning the moldings, and set it on your work table. Cut off a 4 to 5-inch piece of masking tape and apply half the length to one molding as shown, pressing down firmly. Apply tension to the other end of the tape as you pull it around the corner and press it firmly on the other molding. The tape broke? Remove it, cut off another length, and apply with less tension.

Apply tape across the top and bottom of the corner in the same manner, as much as is needed to hold the joint tight. Then assemble the other three corners.

(Continued on next page)

. . . Continued from page 85

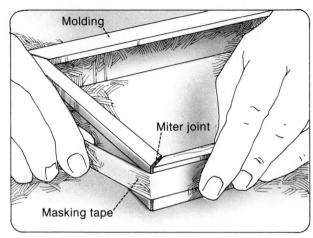

Press end of masking tape onto molding. Stretch tape around corner and press onto other molding.

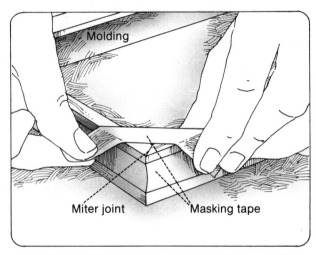

Stretch masking tape across top and bottom of corner as needed to hold miter joint tight.

Nailing and setting. There are framers who maintain that the only function of nails is to hold the joint until the glue dries. Others maintain that nails provide additional mechanical strength. Theoretically a well-glued joint is stronger than the wood adjoining. But nails do give an added sense of security, particularly for heavy objects such as mirrors and for very large frames.

Now that all four corners are glued and clamped, select some brads (or finishing nails for heavier, wider frames). They should be long enough to reach through the different widths along the miters. The best way to choose the right lengths is to lay some nails across the corners, parallel to one side of the frame, and "eyeball" them. Brads or nails of differing lengths can be used in the same corner, though the project is easier if they are all the same length.

Where to nail? In most cases, only from the bottom and top outside edges. Even though you'll be touching up the scars, they'll still be apparent and these are the least noticeable edges. If the frame is heavy you will need to add another nail or two

from the side. Be careful to select spots that won't have adjacent nails colliding.

You should drill holes for the nails, but holes 25 percent smaller in diameter than the thickness of the nails. Drill all the way through the first miter and part-way into the other. The holes are to keep the nails from splitting the often-fragile wood, made even more fragile by the mitering. Use a crank-type mechanical drill, a push drill, or an electric drill, but wrap a narrow band of masking tape, ends flapping, to the shank of the drill point just where it emerges from the chuck. This offers two benefits: it acts as a depth guide and prevents the spinning chuck from damaging the molding.

Nails will enter more easily if you rub them on beeswax or a cake of soap before you tap them in. With your hammer, tap the nail in until the head is about $\frac{1}{16}$ inch above the surface of the molding. Then use hammer and nailset to tap it $\frac{1}{16}$ inch below the surface.

Touch-up and finishing. With the frame made, the last thing to do is fill the nail holes, perhaps do a little creative refinishing, or finish bare-wood molding.

Touch-up. On prefinished moldings, use wax crayons, matching frame repair putty, or colored repair sticks to hide the scars. The sticks also come in gold and silver. Nail points that protrude can be gently pressed into the frame with a burnishing tool. For bare wood that you will finish after making the frame, use a wood dough or wood putty that will absorb stain.

Creative refinishing. As you become more enamored with doing your own framing, you may wish to alter the appearance of prefinished moldings. Imagination and taste are the keys here. You might paint the panel of a molding to pick up a color in the art. Or you might apply an antiquing glaze to an existing panel to tone down a color. Or you might highlight some of the molding's curved surfaces by rubbing on a gold or silver wax. Most of the materials used for finishing bare-wood moldings (see below) can also be used for altering prefinished moldings.

Finishing bare-wood frames. If you make your frame from bare wood rather than finished stock, you have a variety of creative options. Stains, paints and enamels, varnishes and other clear finishes, antiquing (kits are available), and gilding are all suitable.

Before you apply any of these finishes, prepare the frame. Fill and sand to remove any imperfections you don't want. Some imperfections can enhance a frame by giving a "distressed" appearance; you can even add imperfections, but don't get carried away. You can texture the surface by first sanding with coarse (#80) garnet paper and applying a thick coat of thinned acrylic modeling paste or acrylic gesso. These are available from art supply stores. Use a comb, brush, or what-have-you to develop a pleasing texture.

You will find detailed information on finishes in the *Sunset* book *Furniture Finishing & Refinishing.*

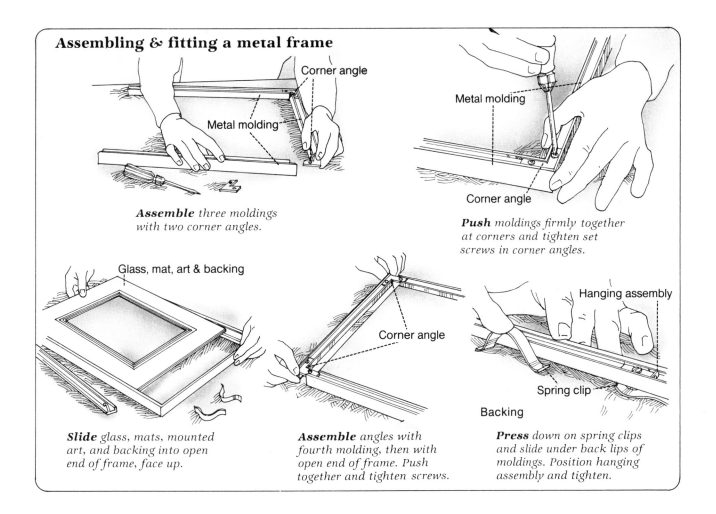

Assembling & fitting a metal frame

Assemble three moldings with two corner angles.

Push moldings firmly together at corners and tighten set screws in corner angles.

Slide glass, mats, mounted art, and backing into open end of frame, face up.

Assemble angles with fourth molding, then with open end of frame. Push together and tighten screws.

Press down on spring clips and slide under back lips of moldings. Position hanging assembly and tighten.

Fitting & assembly

By now, you have gleaned working information on three major components of the frame assembly: the molding, the mat, and the mount. Additionally, you've been exposed to the esthetic enhancements of liners and fillets. It would seem that the picture is well nigh complete, artistically and practically.

But there are still more components for you to consider before you fit the frame together and display your handiwork. Most apparent of these is the glass that adds protection to the artwork, sparkle to the frame, and another capability to your battery of skills. You will also learn to deal with the glass's sometimes surrogate, the acrylic window. Less apparent, but of equal importance, are the backing, the dust cover, and those least visible but infinitely important structural necessities, the hardware by which the picture hangs on the wall.

Tools and materials you'll need. Only a few of the basic tools shown on page 64 are required for fitting and assembly: hammer, nailset or slip-joint pliers, glass cutter and square if cutting your own glass, utility knife, plastic blades for knife if using plastic instead of glass, folding rule or steel tape, and diagonal pliers for cutting wire. In addition, you may need a small screwdriver when fitting canvases.

Also you will need white glue, heavy kraft paper, backing material (see page 55), glass or plastic, 1-inch brads, screw eyes, and braided wire.

Glass & acrylic

As discussed before, most forms of art are framed behind glass for protection. In your pursuit of the framer's art, you will become familiar with glass and its sometime substitute, acrylic. While you can have your materials cut to size at a glass shop, hardware store, or frame shop, you can save many trips and much inconvenience if you cut them yourself.

Pros and cons. Condensation can form behind glass and acrylic both, but to a much lesser extent behind the latter. Acrylic, however, has four disadvantages. Its softer surface is more easily scratched, it holds more static electricity than glass and therefore is a stronger dust magnet, it costs more than glass, and it isn't always flat.

Nonglare glass tends to reduce the visibility of the picture because it transmits less light. Where reflections are a real problem, though, it is a boon. Clear glass, on the other hand, lends an illusion of greater color saturation, especially to photographic reproductions and matte-finish photo prints.

Picture glass is not only thinner than window glass (it is only $\frac{1}{16}$ inch) but is freer of flaws and bubbles. But very large pictures may need single or even double-weight window glass, which is heavier as well as thicker than picture glass. Make sure the frame is strong enough to support the added weight. To reduce weight, you could use acrylic instead of glass.

Measuring and cutting glass. Carefully measure the length and width of the frame between the rabbets—in this case, the frame you made measures $17\frac{1}{8}$ by $21\frac{1}{8}$ inches. Subtract $\frac{1}{8}$ inch from each measurement for the clearance between glass and frame to arrive at the glass size of 17 by 21 inches.

Mark the cutting lines on the glass as you did with the mat on page 73, using the square and a felt tip pen. Lay your straightedge on the glass, aligning it so that the wheel of the glass cutter is on the cutting line. Several pieces of masking tape applied to the bottom of the straightedge will prevent it from slipping around.

Make the cuts as described below, being sure that you don't tilt the cutter to one side or the other.

Helpful hints on cutting glass: Keep the cutting end of your cutter in kerosene or turpentine; they both protect and lubricate. Keep your elbow stiff and step backward as you run the glass cutter. Do not stand in one place and move the tool by flexing your elbow. A steady hiss tells you you're making an easy, clean cut. A "perforation" sound means you are bearing down too hard or that the cutting wheel is dull.

Cut the surface along its full length. Then break the surplus off by hand, unless it is $\frac{1}{4}$ inch wide or less; if so, tap it off with the cutter handle or bite it away with pliers. Don't delay breaking off the surplus, as glass tends to heal itself.

Finally, wash the glass with this solution rather

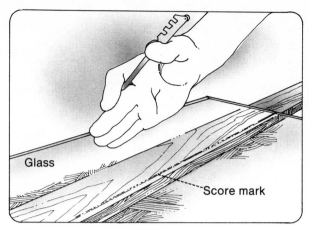

Place score mark over edge of plywood on work table; press down on excess glass to break off.

than a commercial product: Mix a pint of alcohol with a gallon of water, add two tablespoons of rottenstone or whiting and a tablespoon of mild liquid dishwashing detergent. The alcohol and water dissolve grease, the rottenstone or whiting serves to polish the glass, and the detergent is an antistatic agent.

Caution: The edge of a piece of picture or window glass can cause serious injury if not handled with care. This is particularly true when framing with clips, brackets, or similar hardware, as the glass edge is exposed. If using this type of framing, have a glass shop bevel the edges and grind and polish them smooth after you cut the glass to size.

Measuring and cutting acrylic. Though the measuring methods are the same, the cutting methods for acrylic and glass are different.

A plastic cutter is a simple knife with a hooked point. Using the nonslip metal straightedge that guided the glass cutter, draw the knife toward you, using that same rigid-arm stance recommended for glass cutting, and step backward. But you'll have to make several passes, each cut deeper than the one before. Don't try to snap the surplus off until you have cut almost through the material.

Sawing acrylic is best accomplished with a rotating-blade power saw equipped with a metal-cutting blade, preferably carbide-tipped. Jigsaws, saber saws, and band saws will work, but don't exert too much pressure, lest the edge of the plastic melt from the heat. No hand saw is quite right for the job.

Whether knife-cut or sawed, the edge, even though it will be concealed, should be sanded, filed, or otherwise smoothed of burrs that can damage mats and increase the thickness of the edge.

How to fit paintings

Now that you know about the added ingredients that go into a frame assembly, stow them away for a while; the fitting of canvases calls only for one component, the molding.

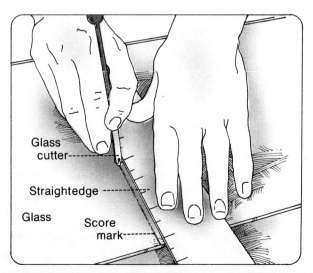

Pull cutter across glass with straight arm and at uniform speed.

You can fasten canvases into frames with metal strips, offset clips, turn buttons, or a combination of screws and screw eyes. If at all possible, be sure to use brass hardware to avoid rust damage later.

If the back of the stretcher and the back of the frame are flush, use strips or turn buttons screwed to the back of the frame. If the back of the stretcher is recessed or protrudes from the back of the frame, use offset clips screwed to the frame, or use a com-use offset clips screwed to the frame, or use a combination of screws and screw eyes (see page 99).

Your hardware store has a selection of metal strips, brackets, and clips. If you can't find exactly what you need, you may find a strip or bracket that you can bend to fit.

All of these systems provide for easy, safe removal of the stretcher from the frame, should the canvas have to be tightened or should you want to change frames to suit a new location or a new owner or the dictates of fashion. It's even possible you'll want to transport the canvas without the heavy frame.

The expediency of stapling or toenailing a stretcher to a frame is disastrous. When you have to separate the two, careful as you are, you'll find it almost impossible not to damage both.

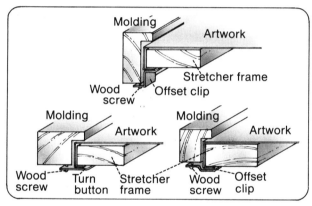

Clips or turn buttons hold stretched canvas art in frame.

How to assemble other art

This section covers the assembling of artwork (other than oil and acrylic on canvas) with the rest of the framing components. As you will see, now is not the time to abandon the care with which you've been working.

The backing. In framing art other than oil and acrylic paintings, yet another decision confronts professionals and amateurs. Whether or not to use a *backing* if the artwork has been mounted. The backing is the final layer of the sandwich that is laid into the frame before the dust cover is sealed on. It both stiffens and protects. If the framing is *archival* (see page 72) the decision is made for you: any extra protection against injury you can provide the art should be supplied.

But a lesser-valued work deserves no less buffering from a fall against the corner of a table or any other threat from the back. You should, then, decide in favor of cutting a backing. Double-faced corrugated board will absorb impacts. It also serves to pad the artwork from the brads, the glazier's points, or those $5/16$-inch staples (used by professionals) that keep the sandwich intact.

For archival work, however, the corrugated board is too high in acid content. You can substitute regular matboard as a stiff backing, provided you place a sheet of nonporous material—plastic food wrap, for one—between the backing and the ragboard mount. A backing of neutral pH board would be ideal and would not require the barrier.

Assembling the framing. "Crabs" are what professionals call those specks of sawdust and other motes they discover inside a finished frame job just minutes before the client is due to pick it up. Threads and lint from fabric-covered liners or mats also make pros crabby. Sometimes they encounter an insect staring at them, looking forward to being framed in perpetuity. Getting crabs out after the frame is locked up is considered a nuisance by some, a reason to change vocations by others. Making sure they are hustled away before assembly is infinitely easier. Also, there is another step you might want to take: adding a component to make the frame airtight so that the frame will remain crab-free after hanging for some time. A potential airway exists between the glass and the molding. To begin with, the rabbet must be perfectly free from splinters and dried glue to provide a stress-free seat for the glass. The extra security measure you might want to take is to isolate the glass from the rabbet.

To do this, cut four narrow strips of matboard—sufficiently narrower than the rabbet that they cannot be seen from the front. They should be as long as each side of the rabbet. Place them on the rabbet with a very light touch of adhesive here and there. These strips become a gasket between the glass and the molding. Now you can set the scrupulously clean glass over the strips.

Next, look at the mat. If it's fabric-covered, check for spots or stains. If it has been well protected during your project's tenure, chances are any spots can be brushed away. Look for flattened places on velvet nap and brush them upright, but gently.

Marks on the mat—a fingerprint, a pencil streak, pastel dust from the drawing—should be carefully removed with an artgum eraser, silicone powder cleanser, a kneaded charcoal eraser, or a kneaded rubber eraser, all available at art supply stores. Test each erasing medium on scrap matboard. You'll find that the gentle, patient touch will work best.

After assuring yourself the mat is clean on its face and that there are no loose particles on its back that might migrate to the artwork, lay it on the glass. Next comes the print on its mount-board. Lift the print gently on its hinges and clean off the mount.

(Continued on next page)

. . . *Continued from page 89*

An aerosol dust-blower that photographers find indispensable is handy for this.

Satisfied that the mount and print are pristine, check the backing for dust, lay it in place, take a deep breath, and prepare to secure the entire assembly. But don't reach for those fasteners yet. Hold the loose components together with your hands and stand it up to make sure no crabs entered while you weren't looking. Also take the time to check that all components are straight and make whatever adjustments may be needed.

Fastening methods. Even if you opted for the airtight gasket for the glass, air remains in the assembly—and it should. There is a tendency to press down on the backing as if to squeeze out all the air. True, some light pressure is needed to make the assembly firm and, in shallow frames, to make room for the fasteners. But too much pressure keeps the artwork from expanding and contracting because of temperature changes and as it absorbs or evaporates environmental moisture, which cause the art to buckle.

Bearing this admonition in mind, you are ready to secure the frame components. Press, do not pound, a ⅝-inch number 18 brad into the midpoint of each vertical inside edge of the molding. The easiest way to start a brad is to push it into the soft backing board at a 45-degree angle with a pair of pliers. The backing board now holds the brad for you. Press it down to a less-sharp angle. The brad should enter the molding only part way. Try one of these methods to press it into the wood:

1) Use one side of the square handle of a nailset and press against the opposite side with your thumb, bracing the outside edge of the molding with your other hand.

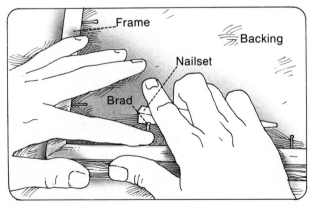

Press brad in *with square end of nailset.*

2) If the molding is narrow enough, squeeze the brad part-way in with pliers. Be sure to protect the visible edge of the molding by padding one jaw of the pliers.

3) Use a brad-pusher. This tool looks like an awl, but its business end has a depression that holds a brad. Remembering to brace against the outside edge, simply push the brad part-way in.

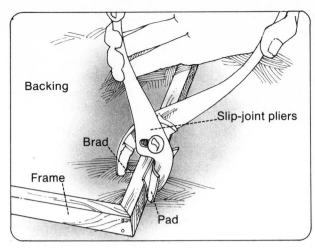

Pad one jaw *when using slip-joint pliers to press brads into molding.*

4) And, of course, you can tap the brads into the molding with a tack hammer. Work against the block clamped to the bench as shown. You can use this same block with the nailset handle and the brad-pusher, too.

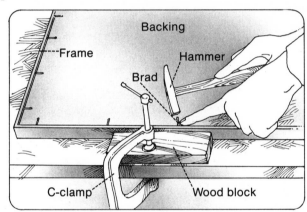

Tap brad *into molding with tack hammer.*

Before you press in the rest of the brads, make one last inspection from the front of the frame. If everything is in place, press the rest of the brads in, 4 or 5 inches apart, working from the center of each side toward the corners. Then with the blunt end of a nailset, press down the ends of any brads that stick out from the backing.

Installing the dust seal. Here is a popular method that is effective and potentially long-lasting, barring damage. Cut a length of kraft paper somewhat larger than the frame. Lay it on the workbench and dampen the side that will face the frame. Run a narrow, sparing, but continuous bead of all-purpose white glue along the back edge of the frame and lay it atop the kraft paper. Lift it and press the edge so that a complete seal is formed. The paper will shrink taut as it dries. Then, with the frame face-down, trim the surplus paper with a knife.

Another version of this same method entails the use of dry kraft paper, and you won't have to wait for the paper to dry. Run lengths of double-coated tape completely around the back edges of the frame so that one edge of the tape is set in $\frac{1}{16}$ inch from the outer edge of the frame. Lay the frame on the paper, pick it up, and press firmly all the way around. Trim as in the first method.

Hanging hardware

At the bottom of this page are examples of the veritable potpourri of hardware available for hanging a picture. However, the strongest, best-concealed system is the standard screw-eyes-and-braided-wire combination on the back of the picture and a picture hook or small nail driven into the wall. Ideally, screw eyes should be installed one-third of the distance from the top of the frame.

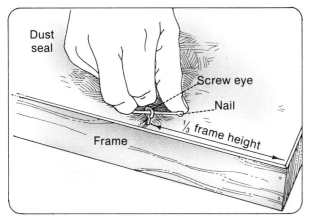

Screw eye *is easy to turn with nail through eye.*

With an awl, make starting holes for the screw eyes. Thread the wire through the eye and wrap the end in a tight spiral close to the eye. Leave enough slack in the wire so that the apex is one-sixth of the distance from the top of the frame—halfway between the location of the screw eyes and the top. Then thread the wire through the opposite eye and wrap as before.

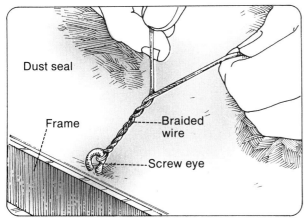

Thread wire *through eye and twist.*

For very heavy frames, install two more screw eyes in the bottom edge of the frame, each one in about one-third the distance from the sides. Fasten one end of the braided wire to a screw eye on the bottom of the frame. Thread the other end through the screw eyes on the frame sides as shown. Then fasten the end to the remaining screw eye on the bottom.

On the wall, two hooks are always better than one. They divide the load and help assure more level-hanging pictures.

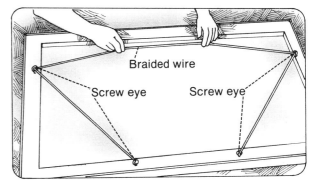

Wire fastened *to screw eyes on bottom gives better support for heavy frame.*

The final touch. Stick two felt bumpers to the back lower corners of the frame. They prevent dust from collecting and provide a flow of air around the back of the frame.

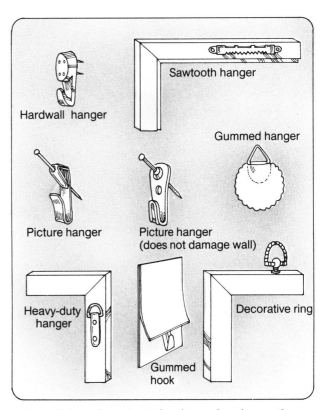

For picture hanging, *there's an abundance of hardware.*

Eight Special Projects

These projects show you how to make some of the frames in the gallery section (pages 4–47) that generally are not available from professional framers. For additional help, refer to "Techniques for framing," beginning on page 63.

Fabric frames

Soft, plush, and brightly patterned, fabric frames lend a cheerful note to favorite photographs or artwork. Fabric-framed pictures make elegant gifts for others or can add zest to the decor of your own home. They're inexpensive to make—and the steps below will take only a few hours of your time.

Here is what you'll need to make a rectangular or square frame with a contrasting inner mat: three medium-weight cardboard mats and three pieces of firmly woven cotton or similar fabric (the one for the inner mat contrasting with the other two). The size of all three mats depends on how wide a border you want around your artwork. As an example, for a 3-inch-wide border all around, you would add 6 inches to both length and width of the picture (in other words, for a 5 by 7-inch picture, the mats would each be 11 by 13 inches). Each piece of fabric should measure an additional 2 inches wider and longer than the mats.

You'll also need enough ⅜-inch quarter-round molding to go around the perimeter of the outer mat; about 2 yards of quilt batting (see Step 6 for precise measurement); masking tape (about ¾-inch wide); white glue; hinge-type clothespins to use as clamps; two small metal or plastic rings (sold at the notions counter in yardage stores); heavy-duty thread; and heavy cord.

1. Cut windows in first two mats (third remains uncut). To cut the inner mat, see "Making mats" on page 70; allow ⅛ inch to overlap your picture. After pencilling window outline, carefully cut it out with a utility knife. Lay inner mat over outer mat, aligning edges. With pencil, trace inner mat's window onto outer mat. Remove cut mat, and mark outer mat for a window ½ to 1 inch larger than tracing. Cut out with utility knife.

2. Center inner mat over wrong side of *contrasting* piece of fabric. With pencil, trace mat window onto fabric; also trace perimeter of mat. Set mat aside. Place tape along inside of window outline, having outside edges of tape touch pencilled lines. Cut out smaller opening inside tape strips (approximately 1 to 2 inches smaller than window outline); snip from each corner of this opening just through tape to tips of window outline corners, forming four flaps. Repeat this step, using outer mat and one of remaining pieces of fabric.

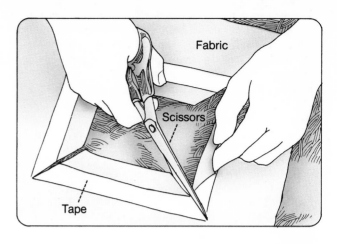

3. Replace inner mat over wrong side of its piece of fabric, aligning window with outside edges of tape. Fold fabric flaps (formed by cutting in Step 2) through window; smooth down and glue to back of mat.

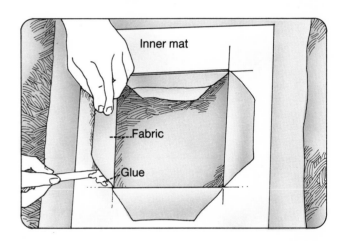

4. Fold outside edges of fabric over outside edges of inner mat; pull taut in back, making sure front is smooth, and glue to back of mat, leaving excess fabric at corners free. Tape fabric to mat until glue dries. Flatten corners and tape tightly, as shown. For an alternative way to cover a mat, see page 76.

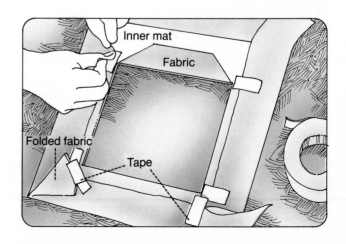

5. Cut molding, mitering corners (see page 83) to fit, rounded side out, along perimeter of outer mat. Glue in place, clamping with clothespins until dry.

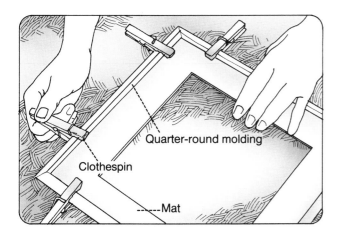

6. For each side of second mat, cut a strip of batting the same length and twice the width. Fold batting in half lengthwise; glue to mat on same side as molding, leaving edges extended slightly over molding.

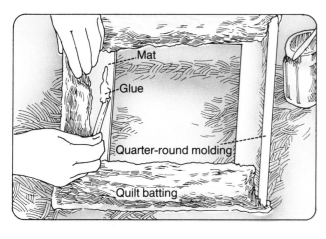

7. Place outer mat, batting-side down, over wrong side of fabric piece cut for it in Step 2. As in Step 3, fold and glue inside fabric flaps through window

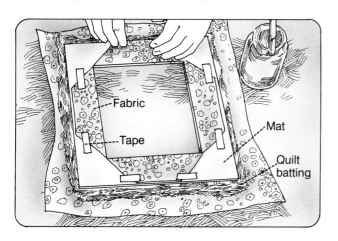

(smoothing them over batting is rather tricky); hold in place with tape until dry.

8. Place inner mat, face down, over back of outer mat, aligning outside edges. Fold and glue outside edges of outer mat's fabric over both mats; flatten corners and secure with tape as in Step 4.

As alternatives, you might cover inner mat with foil, wallpaper, or other decorated paper. If you wish to display picture behind glass or acrylic, cut the material to same size as inner mat (see page 88). Center over outer mat, aligning edges, before putting inner mat in place.

9. Center picture behind window, taping at top to hold it in place. To cover third mat, lay it over wrong side of remaining piece of fabric. Attach fabric as in Step 4, omitting the window-cutting and lining outlined in Steps 1–3. After glue dries, stitch rings to fabric on smooth, taut sides of mats, placing them equidistant from top and sides. Glue third mat, with folded corners facing down, to back of first two mats. Firmly tape mats together, with strips placed every two inches to hold the mats together until glue dries. When glue is dry, remove tape. Fasten braided picture wire between rings to hang picture.

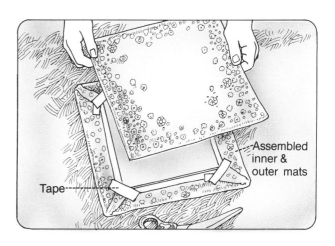

Make your own molding

In the gallery section on pages 10, 25, 30, and 31, you will see examples of frames made from builder's moldings. You will find projects for some of these frames on the following pages. Builder's moldings are those used by carpenters to finish windows, doors and other parts of a house.

The examples illustrated below are but a few of the many frame variations possible, using builder's moldings. The only factor limiting your imagination is the number of different molding shapes that you can find at local building supply dealers.

When purchasing these moldings, select molding lengths that are not warped, bowed, or twisted. Though defects are not serious when building a house, if your moldings are not straight when building a frame, the frame will be badly distorted. Also examine the moldings for knots and pockets of sap. If you find such defects, either select another length or buy enough so that you can make your frame without using the blemished portions.

Making a picture molding from builder's moldings. Here's how to make a frame by combining two or more builder's moldings: Once you have decided on your design and have purchased the moldings, cut a piece of each type of molding for each side, about 2 inches longer than the outer dimensions of that side.

Apply glue sparingly to the narrower of the two pieces being joined and press in place on other piece. With complex moldings of three or more pieces, you may have to glue the pieces together in stages. A wood block, tacked to your work table, may help by supporting one piece while placing the other. (The molding illustrated is the same one used to make the frame for the bark painting on page 10.)

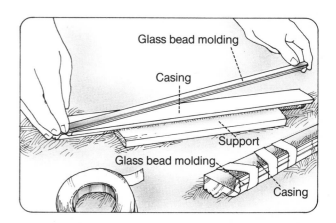

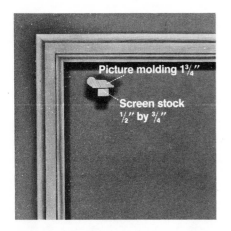

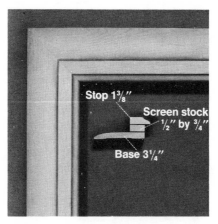

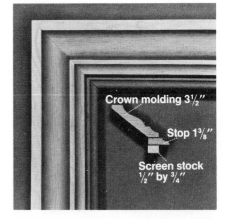

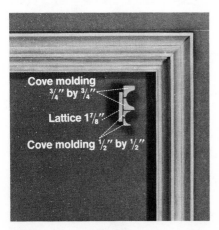

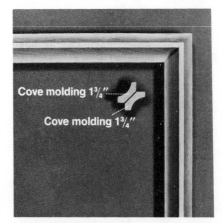

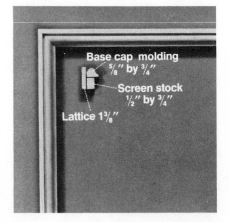

Create your own picture frame molding from moldings used by home builders. Those shown here are typical of the many possibilities available to you.

Wrap the moldings with lengths of masking tape to hold the pieces in proper position until the glue dries. After the glue has dried thoroughly, follow the instructions for making a frame, beginning on page 82. You will find suggestions for finishing on page 86.

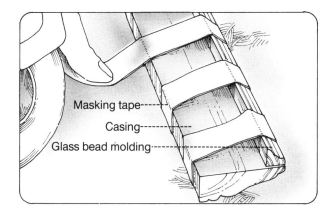

Masking tape
Casing
Glass bead molding

Frame with removable back

The handsome oak frame shown on page 28 was specially designed to house a different poster for each month. Its contents are easy to change because of a removable back that is held in place by swiveling metal strips. This is a project for an experienced

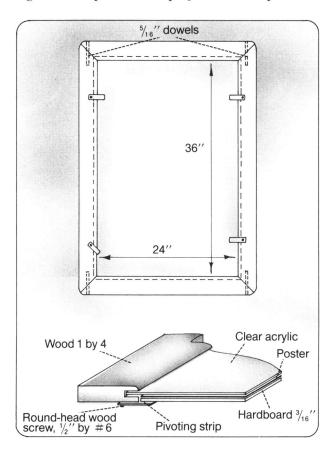

5/16″ dowels

36″

24″

Wood 1 by 4
Clear acrylic
Poster
Round-head wood screw, 1/2″ by #6
Pivoting strip
Hardboard 3/16″

woodworker. Oak is one of the more difficult woods to work, so power tools—table saw, router, and saber saw—will make your task easier.

Though you can adapt this idea to other sizes, the following directions explain how to duplicate the frame shown (which has a 24 by 36-inch opening). Materials you'll need: 13 feet of 1 by 4-inch oak; four 3½-inch lengths of 5/16-inch doweling; a 23⅞ by 35⅞-inch sheet of ¼-inch tempered hardboard; a 24 7/16 by 36 7/16-inch sheet of 3/16-inch clear acrylic and protective paper of the same size; 4 strips of thin scrap metal, each about 2 inches long (or substitute acrylic or hardboard scraps), with a 9/64-inch hole drilled ¼ inch from one end; four ½ inch by #6 round-head wood screws; masking tape; white glue; and Danish oil or other finish.

1. Cut oak into 4 lengths, two at 32 inches and two at 44 inches. With a dado blade in table saw, cut a 3/16-inch-wide groove, ¼ inch deep, along one edge of each length. Groove should be in exact center of edge, running from one end of length to the other.

2. Miter corners (see page 83 for directions), but do not glue. Be sure that grooves will be toward inside of frame when you cut miter. Assemble each corner in miter clamp and drill 5/16-inch holes, 3½ inches deep, for reinforcing dowels, where shown in drawing at left. Label matching pieces for each corner, and remove miter clamp. With a router and a ½-inch rounding bit, round the corners between fronts and inside edges of mitered pieces. Sand the rounded corners smooth so as not to scratch acrylic after assembly.

3. Reassemble one corner in miter clamp, gluing pieces together; immediately coat a dowel with glue and tap into drilled hole. Repeat with one adjoining corner, forming three sides of frame.

4. When glue is dry, slide acrylic sheet into grooves. Glue fourth side of frame to other three, immediately tapping in remaining two glue-coated dowels.

5. Protect face of acrylic with paper and masking tape. Now round the corners to a ½-inch radius with a saber saw or wood rasp and sand smooth. With router and ¼-inch rounding bit, round the front and back outside corners. Sand, and finish with Danish oil or another protective finish.

6. Screw metal strips to back of frame, placing them equidistant from top and bottom (as shown in drawing at left), and with half of each strip extended over frame opening. Screws should be just loose enough to allow strips to pivot. Remove protective paper from acrylic.

7. With metal strips pivoted out of the way, place artwork inside frame against acrylic sheet; place hardboard sheet over artwork. If your poster or other artwork is smaller than the opening, you will need to mount it on a piece of matboard of suitable color cut to the same size as hardboard backing. For information on mounting paper artwork, see page 77. Swivel strips to hold hardboard in place and tighten screws. For information on installing hardware for hanging your frame, see page 91.

Drop-in frame

The mounted art in this frame (illustrated on page 30) slides in through a slot in the top. The frame is made of standard builder's moldings, available at any lumberyard. The dimensions given below fit mounted art that measures $14\frac{1}{8}$ by $11\frac{5}{8}$ inches and allow $\frac{1}{16}$-inch clearance between the mounted art and the sides of the frame.

You will need 6 feet of $1\frac{3}{8}$-inch door stop, 5 feet of $1\frac{3}{8}$-inch lattice, and 4 feet of $1\frac{1}{8}$-inch lattice. Cut this material as follows:

(A) $1\frac{3}{8}$-inch lattice, 2 @ $13\frac{3}{4}$ inches
(B) $1\frac{3}{8}$-inch lattice, 2 @ 14 inches
(C) $1\frac{1}{8}$-inch lattice, 1 @ $16\frac{1}{2}$ inches
(D) $1\frac{1}{8}$-inch lattice, 2 @ $12\frac{7}{8}$ inches
(E) $1\frac{3}{8}$-inch door stop, 2 @ $16\frac{1}{2}$ inches
(F) $1\frac{3}{8}$-inch door stop, 2 @ 14 inches

You will also need a piece of glass, $14\frac{1}{8}$ by $11\frac{5}{8}$ inches, one flat-head wood screw, $\frac{1}{2}$ inch by #6, two small screweyes and braided picture wire, glue, finishing materials, and, of course, your mounted art.

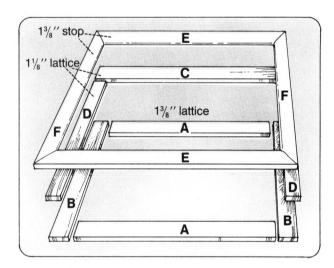

The first step is to glue and clamp the (A) and (B) pieces together making sure that the corners are square. To make the handy miter clamps shown, see page 65. Tie one end of the heavy string (long enough to pass around the frame and clamps at least twice) to the screw in one of the clamps. Position a clamp at each corner of the frame, wrap string twice around grooves in clamps, pull tight and tie other end to a convenient screw. Wipe off excess glue after each step.

Next glue the one (C) and two (D) pieces to the (A) and (B) pieces respectively. Either clamp as shown or hold in place with brads.

Now miter the ends of the (E) and (F) pieces (see page 83 for mitering information). Glue these to the (C) and (D) pieces respectively. Be sure to apply glue to the miters as well as the flat surface of the door stop. Clamp or hold the place with brads. Note that one of the (E) pieces is supported only at the ends.

After the glue is dry, sand and finish the frame. Our frame on page 30 was stained and waxed. You can apply the finish of your choice (see page 86 for information on finishing). Thoroughly clean the glass (see page 88 for glass cutting information). Insert the mounted art and drive the screw through the center of the top (A) piece to prevent the art and glass from accidentally sliding out of the frame. Install the screw eyes and braided wire for hanging the frame (see page 91) to complete the job.

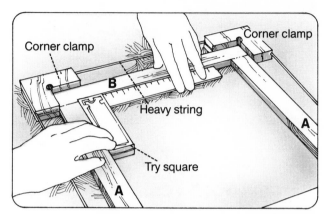

Glue and clamp (A) and (B) pieces; check with square.

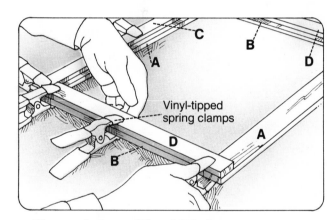

Glue and clamp (C) and (D) pieces.

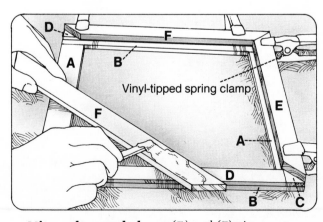

Miter, glue, and clamp (E) and (F) pieces.

Framing a montage

If you are looking for a way to display a picture collection of family members, pets, hobbies, travels, or similarly related themes, you might consider the frame used for the "cattery" shown on page 25. Though some patience is needed when placing the screen mold dividers, the builder's-molding frame is easy to make.

Cross section of montage frame

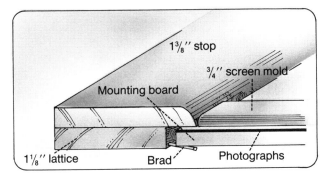

1⅜" stop
¾" screen mold
Mounting board
1⅛" lattice
Brad
Photographs

To make such a frame (ours is 20 by 20¼ inches), you will need some 1⅜-inch door stop mold, 1⅛-inch by ¼-inch lattice, ¾-inch screen mold, white glue, photographic spray adhesive, wax paper, and brads. We used ¼-inch foam-core mounting board, because it is lightweight, but ¼-inch plywood or ¼-inch hardboard can be used too. The exact quantities of materials you'll require depend on your picture arrangement and your frame's overall size.

1. Shuffle your photographs around on a table top or the floor until you have an arrangement that pleases you. The four outside edges of your arrangement must be straight; you will probably have to trim some of the photographs to make them fit into the necessary rectangle.

2. Mount the photographs on the mounting board with photographic spray adhesive (see directions on pages 77 and 78). Be sure to follow the manufacturer's directions, too.

After you have cut the mounting board to size (first step illustrated below), make a frame from lattice and door-stop molding to fit the mounting board (see frame-making instructions beginning on page 82). You will also want to read the information about builder's moldings on page 94. When you have built the frame, follow the rest of the steps illustrated below. Whatever finish you elect to put on your frame, you should do it before you fit the mounted photographs into it (see page 86 for tips on finishing). Information about hardware for hanging your framed photographs will be found on page 91.

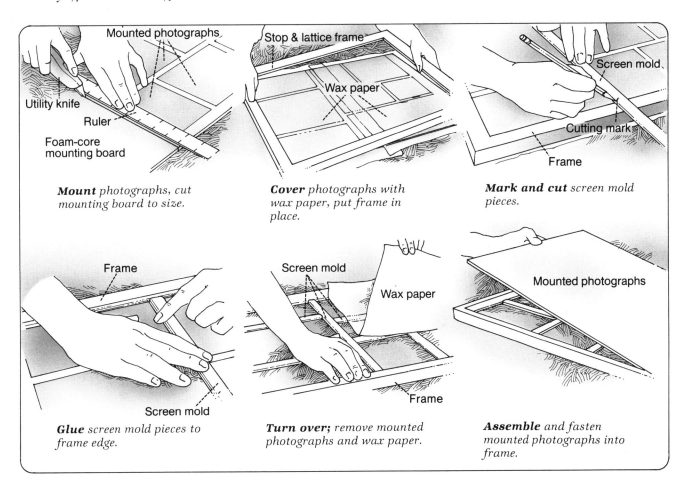

Mount photographs, cut mounting board to size.

Cover photographs with wax paper, put frame in place.

Mark and cut screen mold pieces.

Glue screen mold pieces to frame edge.

Turn over; remove mounted photographs and wax paper.

Assemble and fasten mounted photographs into frame.

Shadow box

Every framer has a favorite way to build shadow boxes so that numerous designs and variations can be seen. The two cross-sections below are variations of the same design. The lower one is illustrated on page 18, and instructions for building the upper one follow. Because its entire box—rather than just the back—is removable, this box can be lined with a single piece of velvet or other fabric, which can provide a lush setting for a fine piece of antique jewelry or works of similar character.

Shadow box & variation

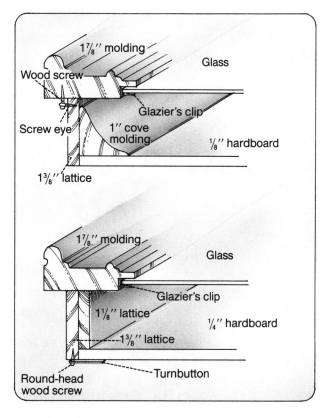

To build this shadow box whose outside frame measurements are 10 by 12 inches, you will need the following:

Combination picture molding, $1\frac{7}{8}$ inches wide, finished or unfinished: 2 @ 10 inches, 2 @ 12 inches.

Lattice, $\frac{1}{4}$ by $1\frac{3}{8}$ inches: 2 @ $8\frac{1}{2}$ inches, 2 @ 11 inches.

Cove molding, 1 by 1 inches: 2 @ $8\frac{1}{2}$ inches, 2 @ $10\frac{1}{2}$ inches.

Hardboard, $\frac{1}{8}$-inch thick: 1 @ $8\frac{7}{16}$ by $10\frac{7}{16}$ inches

6 glazier's clips

6 small screw eyes

4 flat-head wood screws $\frac{3}{4}$ inch by #4

White glue, finishing materials, masking tape, and braided picture wire

Glass: 1 @ $6\frac{7}{8}$ by $8\frac{7}{8}$ inches

Material notes: (1) Check dimensions of finished frame before cutting glass (see page 88). (2) If you use a different width picture molding, adjust the molding lengths so that the dimensions between rabbets of the finished frame are 7 by 9 inches (see information about measuring frames on page 82).

The shadow box is built in two parts: first the frame, then the box.

1. Miter the ends of the picture moldings and glue and join the pieces together (See "Building the frame" on page 82 and string clamp on page 65).

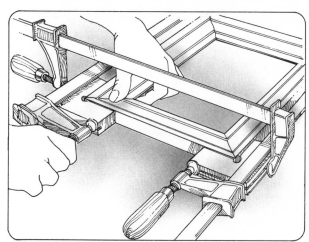

Homemade clamps securing corners are held in place with bar clamps instead of string.

2. Miter the ends of the four pieces of cove molding (see page 83 for information on mitering).

3. Glue the cove moldings to the lattice pieces. Note that the wide edge of the cove is inset $\frac{1}{8}$ inch from the edge of the lattice. This provides a recess for the hardboard back (see cross-section at left). The pieces for the short sides are the same length so the ends should be flush. The coves for the long sides are shorter than the lattice pieces so the ends should be inset $\frac{1}{4}$ inch from the ends of the lattice pieces. Wrap the pairs with masking tape, as shown below, to hold the pieces together while the glue dries.

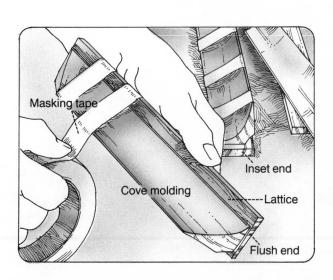

4. Apply glue to the mating surfaces and assemble the sides. Hold assembly together until the glue dries with the wood corner clamps and heavy string used to assemble the drop-in frame on page 96. The masking tape method of clamping corners shown on pages 85 and 86 is a good alternate for joining these corners. Another method is to assemble the pieces without clamps by driving brads through the ends of the long sides into the end grain of the short sides.

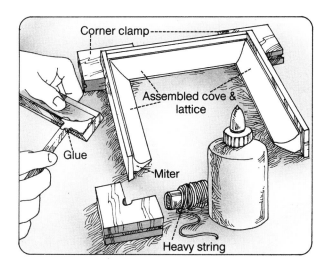

5. Place assembly on flat surface with wide edges of cove moldings facing up. Glue the hardboard back in place, securing with a weight until the glue is dry.

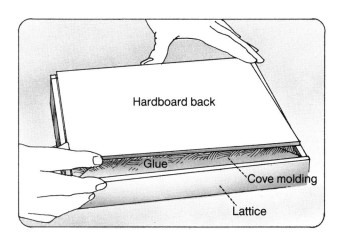

6. After the glue dries, sand and apply your choice of finish to the frame and the box (see page 86 for hints on finishes). The shadow box on page 18 was painted with a base coat and then antiqued with a glaze, a technique that works particularly well with soft wood moldings. If you intend to line the box, do it after the finish dries. Cut and fit the fabric, mitering the corners so that the fabric fits smoothly over the coves. Use glue sparingly when attaching fabric.

7. Install a screw eye at the center of each side, ¼ inch from the edge of the lattice.

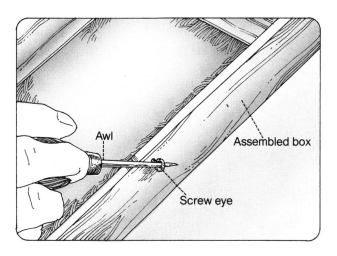

8. Place frame face down on padded surface to protect finish. Install cleaned glass, holding in place with glazier's clips tapped into frame as shown.

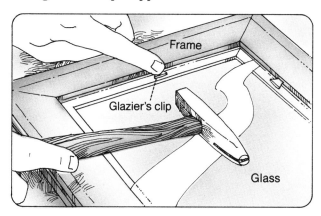

9. Center box, open face down, on back of frame so that distance from box to edge of frame is equal all the way around. Push point of awl through screw eyes to make pilot holes in frame for screws.

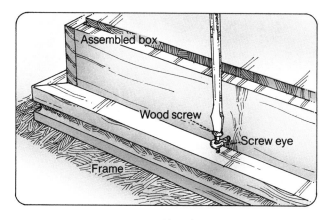

10. Mount your art in box (see page 81 for suggested methods). Install and tighten screws.

11. Install screweyes and braided picture wire on back and a couple of felt bumpers at the bottom corners and you are finished.

Passe partout: framing with tape

Passe partout is an inexpensive, quick method of framing art. Though considered temporary, it can last several years if properly done. Because tape is not as strong as wood, passe partout should be used only with lightweight works, such as the military prints on page 13 or the poster on page 29, prepared for framing as discussed in "Techniques for framing," beginning on page 63.

Some stationers stock tape especially made for passe partout. If you cannot find such tape, you can substitute plastic-impregnated cloth, self-sticking tape, gummed paper, or gummed linen tape. Buy tape that is wide enough to overlap the glass or acrylic cover and the backing by at least $\frac{1}{4}$ inch. *Caution:* Vinyl tapes stretch and are not suitable for passe partout. Also, gummed tapes can be tricky to use: too much moisture will wash the glue away, whereas too little will prevent the glue from sticking.

In addition to the tape, you will need a gummed picture hanger and a few tools: a ruler (or straightedge) at least as long as the longest dimension of the components to be framed, and scissors or a utility knife.

The illustrations in the instructions that follow depict the poster on page 29. Use the same method if framing glassed and matted art such as the military prints on page 13.

1. Check that all the assembled components—glass or acrylic, mats, mounting board, backing—are exactly the same size. One smaller or larger component will spoil the smooth appearance of the tape around the edge.

2. Stack the components in the appropriate order, making sure the edges are lined up, and fasten together temporarily with two strips of masking tape on each side, running horizontally from front to back.

3. Remove strips of masking tape from one side. Position ruler atop components, lined up $\frac{1}{4}$ inch from edge of that side. The ruler serves as a guide when placing the tape. Fix the ruler in position with a hammer or other heavy object.

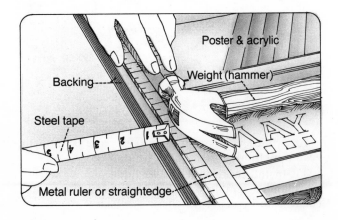

4. Working from one end to the other, apply tape to front of glass or acrylic, lining up one edge of tape against ruler. When tape is in position, remove ruler and smooth tape firmly with fingers.

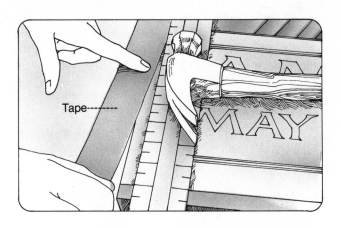

5. Working from center towards the ends, press and smooth tape over side of stack of components and around back. Trim ends of tape flush with ends of components. Repeat Steps 3–5 on opposite side of components.

6. Now apply tape, following steps 3–5, to one of the remaining sides of components, but allow ends of tape to project about $\frac{1}{2}$ inch beyond corners. Slit tape ends as shown in drawing below.

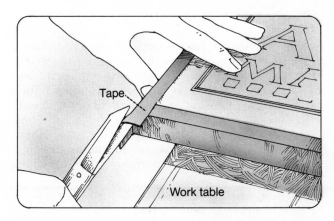

7. Fold the slit tape end over and around one corner, as shown in drawing below. Slit and fold tape end over and around second corner. Repeat Steps 6–7 with remaining side of components. All sides should now be firmly taped and finished.

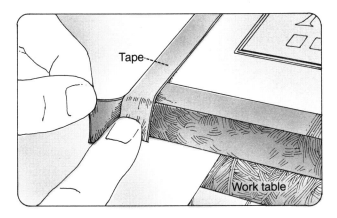

8. Apply gummed picture hanger to back of components; see page 91 for location.

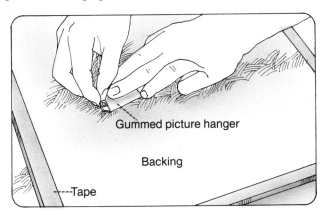

The shoe box lid frame

If your six-year old paints a picture for your birthday, how can you best display it? For one idea, take a look on page 47 at the child's art mounted on a shoe box lid. It's easy to make, inexpensive, and, when the time comes, you can paste a Mother's Day painting right over the birthday gift.

In addition to the shoe box lid (ours measured $7\frac{3}{8}$ by $11\frac{5}{16}$ inches inside—if yours is different, you may need to modify other dimensions), you will need some other materials: four lengths of $\frac{1}{4}$ by $1\frac{1}{8}$ inch lattice, two at $13\frac{3}{8}$ inches and two at $16\frac{3}{4}$ inches; three $11\frac{1}{4}$ inch lengths of $\frac{1}{2}$ by $\frac{3}{4}$ inch screen stock; one piece of $\frac{1}{4}$-inch plywood, and one piece of mat board, both $12\frac{7}{8}$ by $16\frac{3}{4}$ inches. You will also need white glue, 4-penny finishing nails, sandpaper, and finishing materials.

1. Begin by gluing and nailing one piece of screen stock to one surface of the plywood, positioned as shown in drawing above right. Then glue and nail

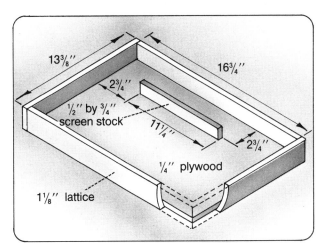

lengths of lattice to plywood edges and to each other at corners. After glue dries, sand and finish the lattice.

2. As shown in drawing below, cut mat board to fit, including a slot for the screen stock, and glue it to plywood surface.

3. Glue the other two pieces of screen stock to the inside edges of the shoe box lid for reinforcement. If you don't have spring clamps like those shown in drawing below, hold the wood pieces in position with spring-type clothespins.

4. Fit art over lid, cutting out corners as shown below, and glue in place. Install screw eyes and braided wire or another type of hanger (see page 91) on the back and hang your child's work in a fitting place of honor.

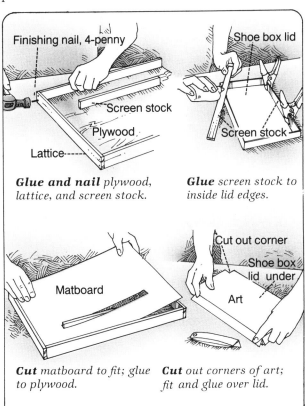

Glue and nail plywood, lattice, and screen stock.

Glue screen stock to inside lid edges.

Cut matboard to fit; glue to plywood.

Cut out corners of art; fit and glue over lid.

For best effect, shed light on your art

You've worked late into the evening to frame your favorite new painting. Or perhaps you picked it up at your custom framer's shop on your way home. You carry it in expectantly and hang it in that special spot you've reserved. Now you can stand back and enjoy it.

Or can you? Something's not quite right; you have to squint to see it. You look around and realize that even though the room is well supplied with lamps for reading, watching TV, whatever, not one lamp lights the wall properly. It's time to think about additional lighting for your pictures and the walls on which they hang.

Patterns of light

A wide choice of light patterns is available to showcase your art. The differences will depend partially on what fixtures you choose, partially on what bulbs you install in them. Your lighting retailer can show you catalogs with diagrams on how the following patterns—and more—are created.

Uniform lighting

To illuminate an entire wall of artwork, there's a pattern called "wallwashing." It can be brilliant or subdued, but it must be even, floor to ceiling, side to side. Wallwashing allows for no areas that are brighter or darker than others.

Nonuniform effects

Suppose the only location for your latest art acquisition is hemmed in by a bookcase. Even though the space cries out for a good-sized picture, it presents a problem: day or night, this niche is dark—the picture will be lost.

But need it be? Not at all. You have a number of options to light this picture selectively, options that will also serve you well when you want to illuminate several art pieces, yet isolate them from their background or from each other.

Let's examine some lighting accents that will work for you.

Spotlighting. To create an impact, highlight your art with the tight oval of light provided by a spotlight. Any fixture that is designed to hold a reflector bulb will accept either a spot or a flood type, since bulb shapes and sizes are the same for a given wattage rating. But with the spot, the light is concentrated and so is much brighter. Like the floods on the next page, spotlights can be used side by side to accent individual pieces of art.

One note: Not all of the smaller—25 to 50-watt—reflector bulbs are quickly available as spotlights. But they are made. Your lighting retailer can special-order the exact wattage you want. In the brighter bulbs that are practicable for picture walls—75, 100, even 150 watts—both floods (designated FL) and spots (SP) are readily obtainable.

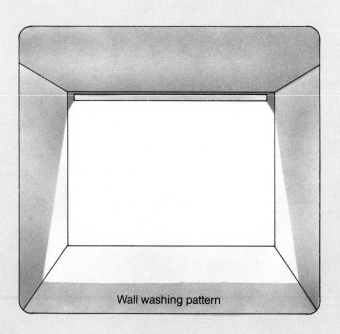

Wall washing pattern

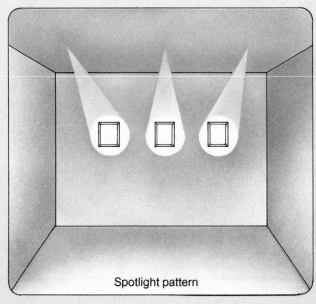

Spotlight pattern

Floodlighting. Paradoxically, a floodlight is a spotlight with a wide beam. But why use a flood to illuminate something that a spotlight will handle? Because you want the light more diffused, or because you want to light some of the area surrounding the artwork to emphasize the picture's role in room decor.

Framed light. Made possible by a *projector lamp* that outlines the art with a rectangle of light, this pattern allows the picture and its frame to "float" on the wall, almost as if they were themselves projected through a color transparency.

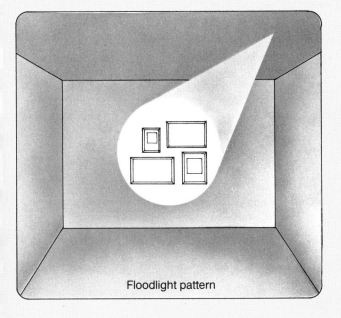
Floodlight pattern

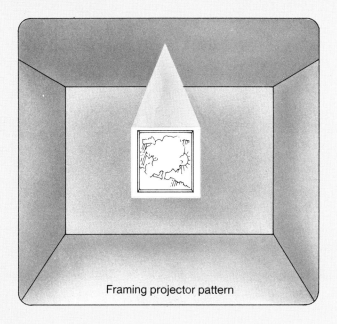
Framing projector pattern

You can even use several floodlights side by side to give each picture in a grouping its own discreet lighting without washing the entire wall with light; just use smaller bulbs. That way you can have all the selective lighting you need without the brightness that will have guests reaching for their sunglasses.

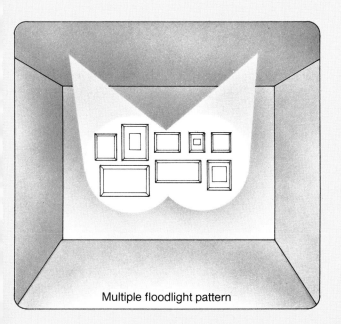
Multiple floodlight pattern

Fixtures

Lighting retailers are universally generous with their advice, and their showrooms sparkle with ideas. You'll find all the lighting hardware you need there.

Recessed lighting. Assuming there is adequate space above the ceiling, and you're willing to cut into it, installing one or more flush ceiling fixtures may be your choice. You should probably seek professional help, though.

Choices for recessed lighting include incandescent or fluorescent, flood or spot, fixed or adjustable, and even a framing light. Ultraviolet radiation from fluorescent lighting, particularly daylight type, is unfriendly to color photographs, but you can buy suitable filters.

Surface-mounted lighting. You may want to consider surface-mounted lighting for its initial economy, ease of installation, or sheer good looks. Surface-mounted fixtures give you great flexibility—you can install them almost anywhere on the ceiling or wall or change from one type of fixture to another.

You have a choice of incandescent or fluorescent, concealed or exposed, or track lighting with a variety of movable spot or floodlight fixtures. And don't forget the classic tubular light in a brass fixture mounted on the picture frame itself.

Index